FOREWORD

Most motorcyclists who witnessed the last few years of Britain as a major producer of motorcycles will remember vividly the impact of one machine in particular, the Honda 750 four. Despite the last ditch efforts of BSA/Triumph and Norton, it was this glittering newcomer that in 1969 showed the direction in which motorcycling was to move through the 1970s.

In 1983, it is difficult to imagine the absence of the four cylinder motorcycle, for years the mainstay of the large capacity bracket. The sheer numbers of Japanese fours is bewildering, ranging from 350 cc and 400 cc Hondas through to the 1100 cc Yamahas. The four has been around long enough now for the buying public to become mildly bored with the whole idea, and has earned the dubious title of UJM – the Universal Japanese Motorcycle. The UJM tag was coined by the motorcycle press in response to the apparently endless stream of fours emerging each year from the Japanese factories, each bearing a close family likeness, even those from rival manufacturers.

It is ironic that the four has been developed, refined and exploited to such an extent that it now threatens to bring about its own downfall through sheer popularity. If an example of familiarity breeding contempt is required, then look no further than the UJM. This curious situation has not gone unnoticed in Japan where a 'new' engine configuration is currently being consolidated. The in-line four will certainly be around for some years to come, but it seems inevitable that the V-twin and V-four are set for a phoenix-like revival in mainstream motorcycling. Honda is at the forefront of this development and currently offers a range of V-twins, threes and fours in their current catalogue.

Just as the four is nearing the end of more than a decade of dominance as the fashionable engine configuration, so before it passed the singles and parallel twins of the 1950s and 1960s. In the western world, few regard the motorcycle as utilitarian transport, and thus designs are dictated not by practicality but by the whims of fashion. Like any other fashionable commodity, motorcycles simply become outdated. I hope that this book will go some way towards placing fours in general, and the CB750 in particular, in perspective.

The writing of this book has been something of a salutary experience. It traces the rise and fall of what was arguably *the* four cylinder motorcycle – a machine that has been loved or derided by many, but certainly could not be ignored. More significantly, it parallels the rise and probable fall of the whole four-cylinder genre, and underlines just how transient a once radical concept seems when reassessed a few years later. It seems probable that the four will become the definitive 1970s machine in the same way that the parallel twin ruled supreme in the 1960s.

I would like to extend my thanks to the people whose enthusiastic help made this book possible. Firstly, Eric Warburton, whose restored CB750 and KO can be seen in many of the photographs used in the book. Eric has spent a great deal of time, money and effort in the course of his restoration work and I hope that the photographs do justice to his hard work. One thing he has shown is that a carefully restored Japanese four warrants serious attention at classic bike shows – he has the awards to prove it. Restoring early Japanese motorcycles is no easy task, the parts being harder to obtain than those for older British machines in some cases, but Eric's machines show that it can be done.

Another enthusiast is Dave Ayesthorpe who owns the automatic and Police models shown in the book. Like Eric, Dave is something of a pioneer in collecting and preserving early Japanese machines, an activity which was the subject of scorn a few years ago but is now being treated seriously. Both of the above are undoubtedly experts in CB750 ownership, and I am indebted for their contribution to the book in the form of the owner interview section.

Colin Gibson is the Membership Secretary and Editor for the Vintage Japanese Motorcycle Club in the UK. His interests extend to all of the historic Japanese marques, but he provided the necessary contact with Eric Warburton and Dave Ayesthorpe, without which the book would have been the poorer. Colin was kind enough to provide the photographs of the original brochures shown in the book.

Finally, thanks to Jeremy Churchill and Chris Rogers for helping with research material and to Bridget Rendall for her help with the research work and her encouragement. Photographs of the CB750 and KO are by Steven Myatt, and those of the CB750A and Police model are by Andrew Morland. *Motorcycle Sport* very kindly gave permission for their road test to be reproduced in this book and also Trent Press (Nottingham) Ltd for permission to reprint Dave Minton's article from the Autumn 1977 issue of *Hondaway*.

HISTORY

To understand the significance of the Honda 750 four, and the profound effect that it and its successors had on motorcycling history, one must go back to the 1960. It was at the start of that decade that the Honda onslaught on the European and North American markets was beginning to have an effect. Progress was slow in the initial years, and though most motorcyclists were aware of the name, few regarded Honda products as 'real' motorcycles. The European and North American manufacturers were largely unconcerned about the newcomer to the business, who pushed ahead with plans to market its then unfamiliar machines.

As has been well documented, Honda sales escalated, slowly but surely, during the early 1960s. Initially, many of their machines were sold to a new market, composed largely of newcomers to motorcycling who were tempted by Honda's successful attempt to change the image of motorcycles in the eyes of the non-motorcyclist. For years motorcycling had been the province of enthusiasts and of those who needed cheap basic transport because they could not afford a car. Many of the latter were swayed by these new machines and the promise of many miles of clean,

trouble-free transport. They were joined by many more new Honda riders, those who had heard that 'You meet the nicest people on a Honda'. By and large, they all found what they were looking for, and Honda sales benefited accordingly.

In a number of boardrooms in the West, complacency reigned supreme. Even if the Japanese had made inroads into the bottom of the market and were persuading people to ride their odd machines, it was felt that the 'real' motorcycle industry had little to fear and that things would stay much as they had in the previous half century. The 'real' motorcyclists were as amused, patronising and dismissive as the companies that built their machines. You might meet the nicest people on a Honda, but not a motorcyclist – not yet.

Attitudes changed slowly during the decade, and Honda slowly but surely began to achieve credibility on the street. The early Dream and Benly models had been around for long enough to prove themselves, and were becoming a thorn in the flesh of the home market producers. The dohc twin CB450 got a mixed reception, but made it clear that Honda were moving up market. The home market manufacturers began to think long and hard, and Honda went racing.

It was possibly Honda's racing efforts that had more impact than their early sales. For years the big European names had battled for status in Grands Prix. Then, in the space of a few years, the names Honda, Yamaha and Suzuki achieved dominance in the racing world as the Japanese works teams and riders battled it out. The technological change wrought by the now wealthy Japanese companies caught the imagination of a new generation of riders. When Honda pulled out of racing in 1967 they left rich memories of Jim Redman, Mike Hailwood and the racing fours and sixes.

Meanwhile, back in the world of the ordinary rider, the ohv

parallel twin reigned supreme as it has for over a decade. The serious motorcylist could be found aboard a Triumph, Norton BSA, Royal Enfield, AJS, Matchless or Ariel. Most displaced 650 cc, one or two had grown to 750 cc and no one suspected what was about to happen. Towards the end of 1968 it was rumoured that Honda were set to launch a '750 cc twin' at the forthcoming Tokyo show, and such rumours were greeted somewhat sceptically. When the rumour changed to the effect that the new machine was to be nothing less than a 750 cc four, developed from the legendary 500 cc racer, scepticism gave way to incredulity, yet on 25th October 1968 it was there for the world to see.

The arrival of the Honda CB750

Soon after its Tokyo debut, the CB750 stole the limelight at a Honda Dealer Convention in Las Vegas. At the convention, which marked Honda's tenth year in the US market, dealers were told that the new model would sell for a little less than the BSA/Triumph triples which with Honda would now be in head-on competition. When in April 1969 the CB750 appeared at the Brighton Show, its UK price was set at £650 – £35 more than the triples. Initial sales in the UK were slow, but not because demand was poor – almost all of Honda's output was being shipped to the USA. To the faltering British motorcycle industry the new Honda must have been a bitter blow. After drifting unconcernedly through the early part of the 1960s, the boardrooms of BSA/Triumph and Norton had at last taken heed of the warnings from their designers and engineers. The belated champions that would fend off any rumoured Japanese invader were the 750 cc triples from BSA/Triumph and Norton's new Commando model. The latter was based on Norton's elderly twin cylinder unit carried in shimmed rubber 'Isolastic' engine mounts which tamed the shuddering parallel twin vibration and resulted in a fast and reasonably light machine. The triples were nearer to being a truly new range and were far more modern in terms of engine design than the long stroke pre-unit Nortons. Both have had their critics, at the time and to this day, but they were undeniably fast and powerful machines.

In a number of the British factories, detailed plans of a variety of sophisticated machines and model ranges had been drawn up. Some of these would have seen the industry through the 1970s and into the 1980s, but both money and foresight were in limited supply. In the rest of Europe, BMW were going through a bad phase in their history, and in any case had never been in the mainstream of motorcycle manufacture. A number of exotic designs were available, even a couple of fours, the Munch Mammoth and the MV, but they were just that – exotic, and beyond the consideration of the motorcycling public. In the USA, Harley Davidson had dismissed their own dohc 1000 cc four because it was felt that no-one would buy such a radical design.

The universal conservatism of the industry prevailed, and everyone stuck to building and selling what they knew best; the British and their parallel twins and the Americans their V-twins. It has been said that the CB750 took less than a year from drawing board to showroom, and whilst this may be somewhat overstated it does indicate what the 'upstart' Honda company achieved. Honda looked hard at the market and saw a possibility that everyone else had ignored. Previously, Honda had gained grudging acceptance by the major manufacturers as producers of entry level motorcycles and mopeds, and as such were considered more of an irritation than a threat. Honda risked a great

deal in committing themselves to the CB750. With one model they intended to leap into direct competition with the industry giants. That they took the risk deserves admiration. The stakes were very high, but they paid off. Honda, and their compatriots, won the lion's share of the world market during the lifetime of the CB750.

In giving the world the CB750, Honda offered the ordinary riders the glamour, sophistication and power that made the western world's finest offerings begin to look a little jaded, if not downright crude. At a stroke, here was a machine with impeccable manners. It was clean and smooth and started at the press of a button, almost as acceptable as a car. Yet it possessed the essential features previously limited to the works racing machines. For years the exotic MV and Honda multi cylinder racers had captivated the racing fans – motorcyclists who would ride to watch their heroes on the inevitable pushrod twins that characterised roadgoing motorcycles. The new Honda arrived almost unexpectedly, and overnight the wildly exotic became affordable to the ordinary motorcyclist. It is very easy to look back on the CB750 as an unremarkable machine, but it can only be considered as such by current standards. To see the model in its true perpective one must view it alongside the machines with which it was to compete – machines which only months before had themselves astonished the motorcycle world.

Time has shown the four cylinder motorcycle to have been a mainstay as were the singles and parallel twins which preceded it. Kawasaki had been working on a four when the CB750 first appeared, and this too became a proven and popular model range. Suzuki joined in some years later, and after initially favouring a three-cylinder unit, Yamaha too fell into line with fours.

Initial fears that the then

exotic engine unit would prove frail and unreliable were later shown to be unfounded, and many owners discovered that they could now spend their weekends riding, rather than repairing, their machines. The unit demanded regular and adequate servicing, but rarely required the costly repairs and overhauls that many had predicted. Handling of the new model was the subject of constant criticism during the early years, and much of this was justified. By European standards it was decidedly lacking in precision, and this reputation stuck. In fact the handling and roadholding could be much improved by the fitting of better quality tyres and rear suspension units, and these formed the backbone of a vast range of 'after-market' items, accessories and modifications which grew up with the model, a subject discussed elsewhere in this book.

CB750

Launched in Tokyo on 25th October 1968, and shown in Las Vegas in January 1969 the CB750 was first seen in the UK in April 1969 at the Brighton show. The demand for the new machine was so great in the USA that few found their way into Great Britain, and there was an initial backlog of orders. There are few known survivors in this country.

The engine was an air cooled single overhead camshaft (sohc) in-line four, the cylinder running transversely across the tubular frame and inclined forward. The camshaft ran centrally across the top of the cylinder head and was supported by four plain bearing surfaces machined in two removable holders and secured by caps. The drive to the camshaft was by an endless chain running in a tunnel between the centre cylinders.

The cylinder head was of light alloy construction and employed two valves per cylinder. The valves were actuated by short rocker arms carried on shafts running parallel to the camshaft.

The cylinder block was also of light alloy construction with extensive finning. It incorporated dry cylinder liners and provided the location for the camshaft chain tensioner and its adjuster mechanism.

The crankshaft was of one-piece forged steel and was supported by five renewable plain bearings. At its left-hand end, the crankshaft terminated in a tapered mainshaft which provided location for the alternator rotor. The alternator assembly was housed in a compartment outboard of the main crankcase but integral with the crankcase castings. Just inboard of the alternator ran the large starter driven gear by means of which the engine was cranked by an electric motor driving through a reduction gear arrangement.

At the centre of the crankshaft, between cylinders 2 and 3 was the single camshaft drive sprocket and the duplex primary drive sprocket, both being integral with the crankshaft. At the right-hand extreme of the crankshaft, the projecting mainshaft end carried the contact breaker and automatic timing unit assembly, these components being housed, like the alternator, in a separate compartment.

To the rear of the crankshaft lay the gearbox input shaft (mainshaft), carrying the five mainshaft pinions plus the large primary driven sprocket assembly. The latter incorporated a transmission shock absorber to reduce drive train snatch. Running parallel to and in mesh with the input shaft was the layshaft (countershaft) and between the two lay the drum-type selector shaft and forks. Drive from the gearbox exited via a pair of final drive pinions to an output shaft and thence to the final drive sprocket.

Also housed within the crankcase area were the clutch,

which was mounted on the right-hand end of the gearbox input shaft, and the kickstart mechanism, which drove the crankshaft via a sprocket incorporated with the primary driven sprocket assembly. The kickstart pinion also served to drive the trochoid oil pump which was mounted at the bottom of the crankcase assembly.

The crankcase castings were of light alloy construction and were arranged to separate horizontally to minimise oil leakage problems. On the underside of the unit a large access hole was closed by a finned alloy cover, whilst the sides of the unit were closed by polished alloy outer covers which contained those ancillaries which ran outside the main casting. It is noteworthy that the lubrication system was of the dry sump type, the engine oil being drawn from and returned to a frame-mounted tank. The oil was passed through a large full-flow oil filter element mounted at the front of the engine unit. This was normal practice at the time, though wet sump designs, being cheaper and easier to execute, have now taken over.

The frame was of welded tubular steel construction, being of twin cradle design. Twin rails ran horizontally from the bottom of the headstock and were joined at the mid point by a larger central spine tube running down from the top of the headstock. The steering head area was gusseted to reduce flexing, as was the area around the rear engine mounts. Front suspension was by oil-damped telescopic forks, whilst rear suspension was by way of a pivoted rear fork supported by twin oil-damped coil spring suspension units. The chassis was one area in which the machine was compared unfavourably with its contemporaries, and was subjected to much detail improvement over the years.

In detail specification the CB750 was equal to or better than anything available at the time. It featured a comprehensive 12 volt

electrical system powered by a substantial three-phase alternator. Instrumentation and switchgear were of a high standard, and it proved that electric starting could be made trouble free, as opposed to some of the dubious arrangements adopted by other manufacturers at the time.

Tuning and competition

Being the first of a new generation of four cylinder motorcycles, it was inevitable that the CB750 model would be raced, and it was quite successful in this respect. As early on as 1970 a factory-backed four man team was entered in the Daytona 200 competing against the BSA/Triumph triples and ohv Harley Davidsons, as well as rival Japanese machines; Dick Mann won at an average speed of 102.69 mph, having qualified at 152.57 mph. Though based on the road machine, the engine was extensively modified and produced 90 bhp rather than the 67 bhp of the production model.

One thing that was shown by the Daytona victory was that the machine was tough, and was able to withstand quite a lot of tuning without any fundamental weaknesses being discovered. It wasn't long until tuning parts became available for ordinary road machines, starting nearly a decade of unofficial development work by the various specialists in the UK and USA.

Companies like Rickman and Dunstall produced complete café racer versions of the machines for those who required something more sporting and individual than that offered by Honda. The Rickman approach was to supply a rolling chassis kit into which the standard (or modified) Honda engine and ancillaries could be transplanted. Included in the kit was a new fuel tank and seat to match the three quarter fairing. The assembled machine looked good, and with the help of Rickman's hand-built plated frame and forks, and Lockheed disc brakes, it handled and stopped very nicely too.

Dunstall retained the Honda chassis, but with modifications in terms of styling and to the engine. The Dunstall Honda was another 'café racer' with a half fairing and a new fuel tank and seat. The Honda four-into-four system was replaced by a Dunstall system designed to extract the maximum usable power from the engine whilst staying within the confines of the 83dbA noise limit then in force in California. The four pipes swept below the crankcase to a collector box which curved back to meet up with the two silencers.

Allied to the fitting of high compression (10.25:1) pistons, the revised exhaust produced enough extra power to allow a 19 tooth gearbox sprocket to be fitted in place of the standard 18 tooth item. Although this gave a theoretical top speed of about 140 mph, it meant in practice that 5th became something of an overdrive gear for fast cruising, and top speed remained much the same as standard.

Other than complete restyling jobs, much could be done by way of tuning and modifying the standard machine. There was soon a wide range of exhaust systems, mostly of the 4-into-1 design, to replace the heavy and rust-prone four pipe system. Big-bore conversions soon became popular with those seeking more power, Yoshimura and Action Four kits being popular and effective choices. The boost in capacity could be enhanced further by fitting a longer duration, higher lift camshaft in conjunction with a less restrictive air filter element. R.C. Engineering produced a good camshaft and K & N air filters are considered a good (and cheap) improvement to the free breathing of the engine.

The chassis was also a target for after-market tuning parts. Some of these could transform the way the machine behaved on the road, notable improvements being taper-roller steering head bearing conversions and phosphor-bronze swinging arm bushes. Also popular were various European tyres and rear suspension units. Many early UK models were soon sporting Girling Gas Shocks and Dunlop or Avon tyres.

In the competition field, perhaps the most extreme development of the 750 engine was in the drag racing specials built during the 1970s. Few can claim to have produced such radical machines as Russ Collins. Having written off a triple Honda engined fueler in 1976 in a 170 mph and $30,000 crash at Akron, Collins returned undaunted in 1977 with a supercharged double engined creation, again Honda CB750 based and making full use of his company's expertise. Lessons learned on the drag strip have provided the basis for R.C. Engineering's range of performance equipment for the CB750.

During the CB750's production run Honda's R & D department did much experimental work on the engine. The latest in a line of successful racing engines bore a close resemblance to its roadgoing counterpart. The major development was a double overhead camshaft cylinder head in which a chain driven idler turned at engine speed at the cylinder head jointing face with gear drive to the two camshafts. The engine provided a valuable test bed, and many of the features developed in it would later be put to use on the road – in the form of the dohc machine which was to replace the ageing CB750 in 1978.

The end of production

By the mid-1970s the CB750 had a lot of serious competition. Kawasaki's dohc four was now well established, and in 1977 Suzuki brought in a direct competitor, the GS750. This, too, had a dohc engine and in terms of performance left the CB750 way behind. Honda responded with the much improved CB750 F2, but this was only a temporary solution.

The old single cam engine had other problems, mostly due to the mechanical noise which made it seem agricultural when compared with the newer machines from rival factories, and threatened to cause problems with the increasingly stringent noise laws.

Perhaps the biggest drawback of all was fashion. The model had been around for a long time now and was no longer able to engender excitement with the buying public. The alternatives were getting better year by year and it was obvious to everyone that a new CB750 would be needed soon.

When it came, the new machine was exactly what had been expected. It showed a hint of the RCB racing engines and of the more recent production engines. It had a new frame which used the engine unit as a semi-stressed member, which in turn eased engine removal by allowing the lower frame section to be removed – curing an old CB750 bugbear at a stroke. The frame showed how design concepts had matured over a decade, the new machine being longer and lower with revised steering geometry.

Right through the machine, one thing was apparent; Honda had designed the same machine, for the same purpose but using 1970s technology in place of the 1960s approach. Though everything was new, the original concept was still there, to the extent that the new machine was available in two versions, a four-pipe tourer with wire wheels, and a four-into-one sports model. The new machines were called the CB750K and the CB750F respectively ....

EVOLUTION

This section of the book sets out the sohc 750 four range in chronological order, indicating identifying features and engine/frame numbers. It is interesting to note how *little* the machine changed throughout its production run, a clear indication of the soundness of the original design. Those wishing to pin down an exact model should note that it may prove hard to make a positive visual identification, especially where the early models are concerned and where, as is likely, previous owners have made changes or fitted later components to update their machines. It is advisable for this reason to check the engine and frame numbers against those given here, rather than to rely on paint colour or the appearance of specific components – both may be non-standard. Note that when ordering parts from a Honda dealer it is important to give *both* numbers to ensure a positive model identification.

The engine number is stamped into a raised rectangle on the left-hand side of the upper crankcase, just below the carburettors. All engines carry the prefix 'CB750' followed by a seven digit number. The first production model was CB750E 1000001.

The frame number will be found at the steering head where it is stamped into the frame tubing.

The prefix in this case is CB750, the first production machine being CB750 1000001.

CB750

October 1968: Honda CB750 model launched at Tokyo show. Engine No CB750E 1000001/Frame No CB750 1000001 onwards.

January 1969: CB750 launched in USA at Las Vegas dealer seminar (Engine/Frame Nos as above).

April 1969: CB750 launched in UK at Brighton show (Engine/Frame Nos as above).

This was the 'original' 750 four, and had no model suffix. The machine was available in two colours, Candy Blue Green (paint code AZ) and Candy Ruby Red (paint code CM). The fuel tank carried contrasting flashes edged with pin stripes and raised metal 'Honda' badges. The oil tank cover and side panel were large and angular with a grille near the front edge and a five-side badge showing the Honda wing logo and marked '750' above. A four-into-four exhaust system was fitted, finished in chrome with heat guards on the upper silencers. Mudguards and rear suspension units were finished in chrome. The carburettors were operated by four cables which ran into a splitter box beneath the fuel tank – a system which was modified on K0 and subsequent variants.

CB750K0

The K0 was a transition model, generally similar to the CB750 and grouped within the latter's batch of engine and frame number span. The K0 variants will fall between Engine No CB750E 1044848 – 1045147, Frame No CB750 *?* 1044826 – 1044947.

All other details, paint colours and plating details are as given above for the CB750. Only 36 K0 machines were sold in the UK.

In most respects, the K0 bore a very close resemblance to the CB750, but featured rocker arm and linkage type carburettor bank in place of the cable operated system. This later system was continued through the K series.

CB750K1

June 1971: CB750 (and K0) model discontinued in UK. Engine No 1045145, Frame No 1044942. K1 model introduced from Engine No CB750E 1044813 approximately, and Frame No CB750 1053399. Note that it is the frame number which will positively identify the model and this should be used for reference.

The K1 was largely similar to the original CB750, but featured a number of styling changes. Fuel capacity in the re-styled tank was increased to 3.9 Imp gallons, and a new oil tank, side panels and dualseat were fitted. The side panel badges were changed using a smaller wing logo, above which was the separate '750 Four' legend.

Paint colours were Candy Ruby Red (paint code CM) and Candy Gold (paint code CQ). The front brake caliper was finished in matt black rather than polished alloy, other details remaining similar to the original model.

The main mechanical change was the adoption of a new throttle operating system in which the four cables were replaced by a rocker arm arrangement. The four rockers were attached to a shaft running across the carburettor bank and lifted the throttle valves by way of rods. The assembly was operated by an opening and a closing cable resulting in lighter and smoother operation. This modification helped to alleviate the erratic carburation

TTU 761H   FRAME 1032375
ENGINE 1032640

9

problems which were often criticised on the early models.

The CB750's appetite for chains was, by contemporary standards, prodigious. The K1 featured a chain oiler arrangement in the output shaft which could be regulated by means of a screw in the centre of the shaft end.

The front fork was modified very slightly and now used a seal of 2 mm larger diameter retained by a 50 mm circlip instead of the previous 47 mm type. Rear suspension was uprated slightly to improve handling, by fitting a heavier spring to the De Carbon type nitrogen-filled damper units. The front wheel hub was reduced in width by 4 mm, and the rear wheel shock absorber rubbers were modified. Other minor changes were to the centre stand, which had a wider left-hand foot, and to the instruments, which now had black faces and glass lenses.

CB750K2

January 1972: CB750K1 discontinued in UK circa Engine No CB750E 1113594, Frame No CB 750 1114090. Replaced by CB750K2 model, Engine No CB750E 2000001, Frame No CB750 2000001 onwards.

The K2 was a minor cosmetic update of its predecessor with only detail changes and a new paint colour differentiating the two. The instrument panel now featured a small centre console housing the warning lamps, and the fork shrouds/headlamp brackets were chromium plated instead of having the earlier painted finish. The new paint colour was Candy Gold Custom (paint code LX). A small compartment beneath the dualseat held the owners handbook plus any other documents that the owner wished to carry, along with helmet hooks. The seat could now be locked shut for security.

Minor changes on the K2 were as follows: A new brake pedal was fitted, identifiable by a small stop on its inner face. The rear wheel sprocket was secured by nuts and studs, rather than bolts, to its carrier. New handlebar switches were fitted, the left-hand component incorporating a small button which cancelled the newly-installed turn signal bleeper. The handlebar clamps were replaced by the one-piece unit incorporating the warning lamps mentioned above.

CB750K3

The CB750K3, K4 and K5 variants will not be found in the UK. These were little more than detail updates of the K2 model, which was retained in the UK until the introduction of the K6.

Another variation of the 'K' theme, the K3 model featured new rear suspension units with modified damper valves and 5 position spring preload adjustment. On the front disc brake, a small shroud was added to help fend off water. Electrical modifications saw the adoption of a more comprehensive fuse arrangement, modified switch gear and a clutch interlock switch. In the engine, new oil ring assemblies were fitted.

A new front fork was fitted this being of the unbushed type with the lower legs sliding directly over the stanchions.

CB750K4

Only the very observant could differentiate between the K3 and K4 models – the latter had redesigned fuel tank stripes! Not imported into the UK.

CB750K5

On K5 versions, the fuel tap migrated from the right-hand side of the tank to the left, and was of a modified design. The friction adjuster on the throttle twist-grip was dropped, and was sorely missed by a few owners. A new side stand featured the now-familiar rubber pads. New turn signal lamps were fitted. (Not imported into the UK).

CB750F

The CB750F was an early version of the F1 model, and was sold in the US for about six months until the latter was introduced. It is generally similar to the F1 and as such is often grouped with it rather than as a separate model type. See following text.

CB750F1

Introduced at Engine No CB750E 2515094/Frame number CB750 1020712 in October 1975, the F1 model was imported until October 1977 by which time it had been replaced by the much improved F2. Final Engine number was CB750E 2563530/Frame number CB750 1040666.

The 750's age was beginning to show by 1975, and the F1 was a serious effort to bring the model up to date. Attention was given to power output, which had dropped off over the years due to the ever more stringent anti-pollution laws.

The new 'F' model actually looked different from its predecessors, and featured a four-into-one exhaust system. The four pipes swept down into a collector box beneath the crankcase, from which emerged the single silencer on the right-hand side of the machine. A new tank was fitted, being more angular than the 'K' type, as were the side panels. A new dualseat featured a tail hump. At the front end, new forks with exposed stanchions contributed to the new 'sporty' appearance of the four. The tank bore the legend 'Super Sport' beneath the Honda badge, and the Honda wing logo had vanished from the side panels. A rear disc brake replaced the drum unit of the K models.

Less obvious differences were the modified front disc brake assembly, and an engine breather element housed in a canister. The element could be removed for cleaning. The swinging arm was modified, as were the front forks and rear suspension units. Other changes were to the instruments and headlamp mountings, the main (ignition) switch now residing in the instrument console.

An endless final drive chain was fitted, along with a modified swinging arm. The grease nipples that were fitted to either end of the swinging arm were replaced by a single central item.

CB750K6

Introduced in the UK in June 1976 to take the place of the old K2 which had been dropped in December 1975. The original plan was that the F1 would have been the K2's replacement, but public demand persuaded Honda UK to retain a 'four pipe' touring version. Engine number CB750E 2438827/Frame number CB750 2573735 onwards.

The K6 model saw the disappearance of the final drive chain oiler, a new plain output shaft being fitted in place of the previous type. The endless final drive chain and the new F1 type swinging arm were also fitted to the K6. Detail changes were made to the carburettors, the throttle stop screw being relocated on the right-hand side of the instrument bank, along with jetting changes. The clutch was modified, the drum being secured by a 40 mm circlip. There were minor changes to the breather hose routing and to the fork top yoke clamp bolts, these being reduced to 7 mm from 8 mm.

CB750K7

Engine No CB750E 271995, Frame No CB750 2719935 to Engine No CB750E 2736452, Frame No CB750 2735472. This was an improved version of the K6 and was first imported into the UK in May 1977.

The CB750 K7 was equipped with the F1 engine unit, and sported new carburettors in which the rocker arm mechanism was contained within the carburettor body. An important feature was the accelerator pump which helped compensate for the otherwise weak fuel/air mixture. A new final drive chain featured, this time of sealed O-ring construction. A label on the rear wheel spindle drawbolts indicated the usable range of the chain. The new chain could not be removed by splitting it – it was now necessary to remove the swinging arm assembly to allow the chain loop to be released. Rear wheel size was reduced to 17 inch.

CB750K8

The very last of the sohc 'K' models, the K8 was not imported into the UK. It was very similar to the K7, serving as a stop-gap model until the dohc replacement was available.

CB750F2

Introduced in the UK in June 1977, the F2 ran from Engine No CB750GE 1000016 to 1012651, Frame No CB750G 1000014 to 1015084. The most powerful of the sohc 750s, the F2 remained available until May 1979, in the UK.

This was to be the final incarnation of the sohc CB750, and

by now everyone knew that a new dohc model was on the way. The only real question was when. It is easy to dismiss the F2 as a cosmetic stop-gap, but in truth it was quite extensively modified. The machine certainly looked newer, featuring the controversial Comstar wheels with pressed artillery spokes riveted to alloy rims. The venerable engine was given a coat of black paint in place of the usual lacquer. Styling was much the same as the F1, but with a new paint scheme.

Beneath the surface lay the real changes. A new cylinder head featured larger inlet tracts, now 32 mm rather than 30 mm, with the inlet valve diameter increased from 32 mm to 34 mm. Exhaust valves grew 3 mm in diameter to 31 mm. A new, higher lift, camshaft combined with the above to up the power to 72 bhp. To cope with the extra power, the crankshaft, main bearings, cylinder head studs and cylinder block were all uprated, as were the clutch springs.

The chassis was also uprated to match the intended sporting image, and now came with twin front disc brakes, the calipers having been completely redesigned. Suspension was tauter than on the previous model.

The F2 was a respectable performer, well able to hold its own with the competition, almost a decade on from the original model. Its purpose was to maintain credibility for the CB750 until its twin-cam successor was ready. That it was able to do so speaks volumes for the design of the machine which shook the motorcycle world in 1968.

CB750F3

Supplied to the US market, the F3 ran from Engine No CB750E 3100002 to 3157915, Frame No CB750F 2200001 to 2257915. It is generally the same as the F2.

CB750A

1976 model, Frame No CB750A 7000000 onwards
1977 model, Frame No CB750A 7100000 onwards
1978 model, Frame No CB750A 7200000 onwards

The CB750A was a radical departure from orthodox motorcycle design, being one of a very small number of machines to offer automatic transmission in place of the conventional foot gearchange arrangement. The engine itself was generally similar to the other CB750 models, but all transmission components were unique to the CB750A.

The conventional wet multi-plate clutch was replaced by an automatic type torque converter. Oil was fed to the converter from the duplex oil pump, via a regulator valve unit. Two drive ratios were available, each comprising a pair of gears working in conjunction with two independent, hydraulically-operated, clutches.

A foot selector pedal allowed the rider to engage neutral, low or drive as required, these being indicated on the instrument panel by lamps marked 'Neutral', '1' and '2' in the case of the later models, or 'Neutral', 'L' and 'D' in the case of the '76-'77 versions. An interlock arrangement ensured that the machine was in neutral whenever the side stand was in use, to prevent the machine's unexpected departure under the effects of automatic transmission 'creep'.

A parking brake, operated by a cable terminating in a knob similar to those normally used on choke controls, allowed the machine to be parked safely on hills or to hold the machine against the tendency to creep at junctions.

In use, the machine was, as could be expected, easy to ride, the low ratio being particularly useful in town or in hilly country. The CB750A found a limited market, however, and the majority of riders considered it to be at odds with their concept of what a motorcycle should be.

An evaluation model was sent to the UK, but after the market had been tested with the 400 cc twin automatic it was felt that the larger model had no market on this side of the Atlantic.

SPECIFICATION

There follows details on the basic specifications of the various CB750 sohc models. Though Honda have not released the numbers of each model manufactured, it is interesting to note that approximately 620,000 sohc CB750 models were produced.

Type designation	Honda CB750, CB750K0
Engine	
Type	Air cooled four cylinder four stroke, sohc
Bore and stroke	61 x 63 mm
Displacement	736 cc (44.93 cu in)
Compression ratio	9.0:1
Maximum power	67 bhp @ 8000 rpm
Maximum torque	44.12 lbf ft @ 7000 rpm (6.1 kgf m @ 7000 rpm)
Carburettors	4 x 28 mm Keihin, slide type, all-cable, operation on CB750 model only
Transmission	
Gearbox	5-speed constant mesh
Ratios	1st 2.500:1
	2nd 1.708:1
	3rd 1.333:1
	4th 1.097:1
	Top 0.939:1
Primary reduction	1.708:1
Secondary reduction	1.167:1
Final reduction	2.667:1 (18T x 48T)
Chassis	
Frame	Welded tubular steel
Front suspension	Oil damped telescopic fork, 5.6 in travel
Rear suspension	Oil damped coil spring units, 3.3 in travel
Brakes: front	Single hydraulic disc brake
rear	Single leading shoe drum brake
Dimensions	
Overall length	85.0 in (2160 mm)
Overall width	34.8 in (885 mm)
Overall height	45.5 in (1155 mm)
Wheelbase	57.3 in (1455 mm)
Seat height	31.5 in (800 mm)
Ground clearance	5.5 in (140 mm)
Curb weight	517.3 lb (235 kg)

Super Profile

Wheels
Type — Wire spoked, chrome plated steel rims
Tyre sizes — Front: 3.25-19 (4PR); Rear: 4.00-18 (4PR)

Electrical system
Type — 12 volt, negative (−) earth
Ignition — Coil and contact breaker, spare spark
Alternator — 3-phase, 12 volt 0.21 kW @ 5000 rpm
Battery — 12 volt 14 Ampere-hour

Type designation — CB750K1

Engine
Type — Air cooled four cylinder four stroke, sohc
Bore and stroke — 61 x 63 mm (2.401 x 2.408 in)
Displacement — 736 cc (44.93 cu in)
Compression ratio — 9.0:1
Maximum power — n/a
Maximum torque — n/a
Carburettors — 4 x 28 mm Keihin, slide type

Transmission
Gearbox — 5-speed constant mesh
Ratios — 1st 2.500:1
2nd 1.708:1
3rd 1.333:1
4th 1.097:1
Top 0.939:1
Primary reduction — 1.708:1
Secondary reduction — n/a
Final reduction — 2.667:1 (18T x 48T)

Chassis
Frame — Welded tubular steel
Front suspension — Oil damped telescopic fork, 5.6 in travel
Rear suspension — Oil damped coil spring units, 3.3 in travel
Brakes: front — Single hydraulic disc brake
rear — Single leading shoe drum brake

Dimensions
Overall length — 85.0 in (2160 mm)
Overall width — 34.8 in (885 mm)
Overall height — 45.5 in (1155 mm)
Wheelbase — 57.3 in (1455 mm)
Seat height — 31.5 in (800 mm)
Ground clearance — 5.5 in (140 mm)
Curb weight — 479.0 lb (218 kg)

Wheels
Type — Wire spoked, chrome plated steel rims
Tyre sizes — Front 3.25-19 (4PR); Rear: 4.00-18 (4PR)

Electrical system
Type — 12 volt, negative (−) earth
Ignition — Coil and contact breaker, spare spark
Alternator — 3-phase, 12 volt 0.21 kW @ 5000 rpm
Battery — 12 volt 14 Ampere-hour

Type designation — CB750K2, K3, K4, K5

Engine
Type — Air cooled four cylinder four stroke, sohc
Bore and stroke — 61.0 x 63.0 mm (2.401 x 2.408 in)
Displacement — 736 cc (44.93 cu in)
Compression ratio — 9.0:1
Maximum power — n/a

Maximum torque	n/a
Carburettors	4 x 28 mm Keihin, slide type
Transmission	
Gearbox	5-speed constant mesh
Ratios	1st 2.500:1
	2nd 1.708:1
	3rd 1.333:1
	4th 1.097:1
	Top 0.939:1
Primary reduction	1.708:1
Secondary reduction	n/a
Final reduction	2.667:1 (18T x 48T)
Chassis	
Frame	Welded tubular steel
Front suspension	Oil damped telescopic fork, 5.6 in travel
Rear suspension	Oil damped coil spring units, 3.3 in travel
Brakes: front	Single hydraulic disc brake
rear	Single leading shoe drum brake
Dimensions	
Overall length	85.6 in (2175 mm)
Overall width	34.3 in (870 mm)
Overall height	46.1 in (1170 mm)
Wheelbase	57.3 in (1455 mm)
Seat height	31.9 in (810 mm)
Ground clearance	5.5 in (140 mm)
Curb weight	479.0 lb (218 kg)
Wheels	
Type	Wire spoked, chrome plated steel rims
Tyre sizes	Front 3.25-19 (4PR); Rear: 4.00-18 (4PR)
Electrical system	
Type	12 volt, negative (−) earth
Ignition	Coil and contact breaker, spare spark
Alternator	3-phase, 12 volt 0.21 kW @ 5000 rpm
Battery	12 volt 14 Ampere-hour
Type designation	Honda CB750K6
Engine	
Type	Air cooled four cylinder four stroke, sohc
Bore and stroke	61 x 63 mm (2.401 x 2.408 in)
Displacement	736 cc (44.93 cu in)
Compression ratio	9.0:1
Maximum power	n/a
Maximum torque	n/a
Carburettors	4 x 28 mm Keihin, slide type
Transmission	
Gearbox	5-speed constant mesh
Ratios	1st 2.500:1
	2nd 1.708:1
	3rd 1.333:1
	4th 1.097:1
	Top 0.939:1
Primary reduction	1.708:1
Secondary reduction	n/a
Final reduction	2.667:1 (18T x 48T)
Chassis	
Frame	Welded tubular steel
Front suspension	Oil damped telescopic fork, 5.6 in travel

Rear suspension	Oil damped coil spring units, 3.3 in travel
Brakes: front	Single hydraulic disc brake
rear	Single leading shoe drum brake

Dimensions

Overall length	85.6 in (2175 mm)
Overall width	34.3 in (870 mm)
Overall height	46.1 in (1170 mm)
Wheelbase	57.3 in (1455 mm)
Seat height	31.9 in (810 mm)
Ground clearance	5.5 in (140 mm)
Curb weight	479 lb (218 kg)

Wheels

Type	Wire spoked, chrome plated steel rims
Tyre sizes	Front 3.25-19 (4PR); Rear: 4.00-18 (4PR)

Electrical system

Type	12 volt, negative (−) earth
Ignition	Coil and contact breaker, spare spark
Alternator	3-phase, 12 volt 0.21 kW @ 5000 rpm
Battery	12 volt 14 Ampere-hour

Type designation

Honda CB750K7

Engine

Type	Air cooled four cylinder four stroke, sohc
Bore and stroke	61 x 63 mm (2.401 x 2.408 in)
Displacement	736 cc (44.93 cu in)
Compression ratio	9.2:1
Maximum power	n/a
Maximum torque	n/a
Carburettors	4 x 28 mm Keihin, slide type

Transmission

Gearbox	5-speed constant mesh
Ratios	1st 2.500:1
	2nd 1.708:1
	3rd 1.333:1
	4th 1.133:1
	Top 0.969:1
Primary reduction	1.708:1
Secondary reduction	n/a
Final reduction	2.733:1 (15T x 41T)

Chassis

Frame	Welded tubular steel
Front suspension	Oil damped telescopic fork, 5.6 in travel
Rear suspension	Oil damped coil spring units, 3.3 in travel
Brakes: front	Single hydraulic disc brake
rear	Single leading shoe drum brake

Dimensions

Overall length	89.8 in (2280 mm)
Overall width	34.6 in (880 mm)
Overall height	46.7 in (1185 mm)
Wheelbase	58.9 in (1495 mm)
Seat height	31.9 in (810 mm)
Ground clearance	5.9 in (150 mm)
Curb weight	508 lb (231 kg)

Wheels

Type	Wire spoked, chrome plated steel rims
Tyre sizes	Front 3.50H-19 (4PR); Rear: 4.50H-17A (4PR)

Electrical system

Type	12 volt, negative (−) earth
Ignition	Coil and contact breaker, spare spark

Alternator	3-phase, 12 volt 0.21 kW @ 5000 rpm
Battery	12 volt 14 Ampere-hour

Type designation — CB750F, F1

Engine
Type	Air cooled four cylinder four stroke, sohc
Bore and stroke	61 x 63 mm (2.401 x 2.408 in)
Displacement	736 cc (44.93 cu-in)
Compression ratio	9.2:1
Maximum power	n/a
Maximum torque	n/a
Carburettors	4 x 28 mm Keihin, slide type

Transmission
Gearbox	5-speed constant mesh
Ratios	1st 2.500:1
	2nd 1.708:1
	3rd 1.333:1
	4th 1.133:1
	Top 0.969:1
Primary reduction	1.985:1
Secondary reduction	n/a
Final reduction	2.824:1 (17T x 48T)

Chassis
Frame	Welded tubular steel
Front suspension	Oil damped telescopic fork, 5.6 in travel
Rear suspension	Oil damped coil spring units, 3.3 in travel
Brakes: front	Single hydraulic disc brake
rear	Single leading shoe drum brake

Dimensions
Overall length	86.6 in (2200 mm)
Overall width	33.9 in (860 mm)
Overall height	45.7 in (1160 mm)
Wheelbase	57.9 in (1470 mm)
Seat height	31.9 in (810 mm)
Ground clearance	5.3 in (135 mm)
Curb weight	499 lb (227 kg)

Wheels
Type	Wire spoked, chrome plated steel rims
Tyre sizes	Front 3.25H-19 (4PR); Rear: 4.00H-18 (4PR)

Electrical system
Type	12 volt, negative (–) earth
Ignition	Coil and contact breaker, spare spark
Alternator	3-phase, 12 volt 0.21 kW @ 5000 rpm
Battery	12 volt 14 Ampere-hour

Type designation — CB750F2

Engine
Type	Air cooled four cylinder four stroke, sohc
Bore and stroke	61 x 63 mm (2.401 x 2.408 in)
Displacement	736 cc (44.93 cu in)
Compression ratio	9.0:1
Maximum power	n/a
Maximum torque	n/a
Carburettors	4 x 28 mm Keihin, slide type

Transmission
Gearbox	5-speed constant mesh
Ratios	1st 2.500:1

	2nd 1.708:1
	3rd 1.333:1
	4th 1.133:1
	Top 0.096:1
Primary reduction	1.708:1
Secondary reduction	n/a
Final reduction	2.824:1 (17T x 48T)
Chassis	
Frame	Welded tubular steel
Front suspension	Oil damped telescopic fork, 5.6 in travel
Rear suspension	Oil damped coil spring units, 4.0 in travel
Brakes: front	Twin hydraulic disc brake
rear	Single hydraulic disc brake
Dimensions	
Overall length	87.0 in (2210 mm)
Overall width	33.9 in (860 mm)
Overall height	46.7 in (1185 mm)
Wheelbase	58.3 in (1480 mm)
Seat height	32.7 in (830 mm)
Ground clearance	5.3 in (135 mm)
Curb weight	512.6 lb (232.5 kg)
Wheels	
Type	'Comstar' composite construction
Tyre sizes	Front 3.25H-19 (4PR); Rear: 4.00H-18 (4PR)
Electrical system	
Type	12 volt, negative (–) earth
Ignition	Coil and contact breaker, spare spark
Alternator	3-phase, 12 volt 0.21 kW @ 5000 rpm
Battery	12 volt 14 Ampere-hour

Type designation	CB750A
Engine	
Type	Air cooled four cylinder four stroke, sohc
Bore and stroke	61 x 63 mm (2.401 x 2.408 in)
Displacement	736 cc (44.93 cu in)
Compression ratio	8.6:1
Maximum power	n/a
Maximum torque	n/a
Carburettors	4 x 28 mm Keihin, slide type
Transmission	
Gearbox	2-speed automatic, with torque converter
Primary reduction	1.351:1 (1.349:1 '77 and '78 model)
Low (1) ratio	2.263:1
High (2) ratio	1.520:1
Final reduction	
1976 model	2.824:1 (17 x 48T)
1977-78 model	2.800:1 (15 x 42T)
Chassis	
Frame	Welded tubular steel
Front suspension	Oil damped telescopic fork, 5.6 in travel
Rear suspension	Oil damped coil spring units, 3.6 in travel
Brakes: front	Single hydraulic disc brake
rear	Single leading shoe drum brake
Dimensions	
Overall length	88.6 in (2250 mm)
Overall width	34.1 in (865 mm)

Overall height	
1976 model	46.7 in (1185 mm)
1977-78 model	46.9 in (1190 mm)
Wheelbase	58.3 in (1480 mm)
Seat height:	
1976 model	32.3 in (820 mm)
1977-78 model	31.9 in (810 mm)
Ground clearance:	
1976 model	5.3 in (135 mm)
1977 model	5.5 in (140 mm)
Curb weight	
1976 model	531 lb (241 kg)
1977 model	534 lb (242 kg)
1978 model	540 lb (245 kg)
Wheels	
Type	Wire spoked, chrome plated steel rims
Tyre sizes	Front 3.50H-19 (4PR); Rear: 4.50H-17A (4PR)
Electrical system	
Type	12 volt, negative earth
Ignition	Coil and contact breaker, spare spark
Alternator	3-phase, 12 volt 0.29 kW @ 5000 rpm
Battery	12 volt 20 Ampere-hour

ROAD TESTS

HONDA 750-4

"Bread-and-butter" Superbike?

IN YEARS to come, when historians look back on the revival of motorcycling and the motorcycle in the 70s, one of the turning points will be seen as the day when Honda made one of the most sophisticated, supposedly complicated and certainly potent, motorcycles available to the general public at a price it could afford. Since then others have joined in the game. Now there are faster bikes, more expensive bikes, bikes with more cylinders but none have sold like the Honda 750. Thousands have poured into every motorcycle-importing country in the world and there have been very few disenchanted owners.

How did Honda succeed when others failed?

Timing, of course, was all important. They made the glamorous four desirable with a string of racing successes and, judging the mood of the market to perfection, they then offered it to the motorcyclist at a price that was at least thinkable. The result was a boom in not only Honda sales but in those of every other manufacturer of big bikes. I think most sectors of the motorcycle industry recognise their debt to Honda for stimulating an ailing market.

That was long enough ago for the Honda "750-4" to be taken for granted on our roads today. It was also long enough ago for fashions to have changed (come to think of it yesterday was long enough ago for that!). Bikes have become more economy-minded, performance is no longer the only criterion a rider uses when buying a machine, and now he can choose from an array of like-capacity bikes. Yet, after all this time the Honda has hardly changed at all, at least to outward appearances. They are even still using at least one of the colour schemes they displayed some years back, a not particularly eye-catching gold.

Internally, we are assured, little of the original engine remains unaltered, a situation any dealer will readily endorse as he struggles to keep up with the spare parts lists. The basic concept of the setup is as before, with an air-cooled, chain-drive-overhead-camshaft, in line four-cylinder engine, differing from the Kawa-saki tested last month in having one camshaft less, and a slight tilt forward. Bore is 61mm and stroke 63mm, giving a total cylinder capacity of 736 c.c. Compression ratio is 9 to 1. Still retained is the endless camshaft and primary drive chain running from the centre of the crankshaft, but our earlier fears of wreaking havoc and resulting in a complete engine strip down do not seem to have been justified for chain life, aided by running in dirt-free conditions, has apparently been good and we have only heard of one primary chain breakage in the past five years, although we recognise that not every reader is going to write to us mentioning this. We were also bothered by the risk of damage to the protruding alternator on the right hand end of the crankshaft when we rode the bike all those years ago. This has, perhaps, given some riders unlucky enough to drop the bike on that side problems, but again few Honda 750 owners have complained.

Carburation is by four 28mm Keihin carburettors of the piston valve type. They are controlled by a double push-pull cable on a pulley with a bar activating the slides. Externally the engine differs from the original by having larger anti-vibration pillars on the cylinders and different plug caps. The curses as riders dried out the old ones must have been heard all the way to Tokio. Our machine, virtually brand new upon collection, had a

handsome gleam to it with all the engine covers and cylinder fins looking pristine. Soon it was like most Honda 750s that we see around, with the engine block and exhaust system only clean where we could reach. Some riders manage to keep their bikes looking as though they have just left the factory but, frankly, we don't know how they do it. Particularly difficult to keep clean are the exhaust pipes and silencers. The "hidden" silencers are easy to neglect and tend to suffer somewhat. They are very expensive to replace, Honda exhaust systems, and we would like to see Honda, who have pioneered so much that is good in motorcycling, think about stainless steel as an alternative material. One thing about the pipes, they managed to keep their colour, an 8in double thickness from the exhaust flange effectively dissipating heat.

As always, the engine was reasonably oil-tight but a little oil *did* escape from the Triumph-style rocker caps. With such a massive alloy unit it was to be expected that some mechanical noise would be evident. It was what other Four owners described as "the good old Honda rattle"—nothing serious, just the sound of four pistons, eight valves and two chains working in unison ! One sound that has left the bike is the loud screech as the starter-button was pressed. Now it is just a civilised whirr. Not for long, either, for the motor invariably fired instantly, the carburettor-mounted choke lever being used from cold. I *still* prefer a handlebar-mounted choke lever, even if it does mean an extra cable.

The gearbox, five-speed, has always been an area where Honda are just a little less than perfect. They are rarely bad, just . . . ordinary. Our 750 was always noisy when engaging bottom from neutral and one needed time and concentration to achieve quiet gear changes. Naturally our technique improved as the miles increased and clearly an owner would soon learn the trick. The clutch was surprisingly light and just about right for our taste.

The frame appears (which is the key word, Honda often appear to have remained unchanged when the reverse is the case) to have changed little. It is of duplex cradle type with twin tubes along the bottom of the tank and a large-section tube from the top of the steering-head to the rear. There is no gusseting at the front. The rear sub-frame has quite a robust triangular section either side to support the exhaust system and pillion rests. Little yellow blobs of paint are evident on various nuts (as they were on the 900 Kawasaki) to indicate that the nut has been torqued to the correct poundage.

The front footrests are spring-loaded and were, for our taste, a mite too easy to fold, often doing so unintentionally when we returned a foot to the rest upon starting. The dual seat, comfortable and ample, is hinged and lockable with helmet holders now fitted either side. All we have to do now is prevail upon helmet manufacturers to build special locking rings into safety helmets. Which, we will concede, is more difficult than it seems. No adjustment was required to the rear chain during the 500 miles of the test but we will agree that this in itself does not prove much. Chain life is still a major talking point wherever Honda 750 owners meet and we know of some who have transferred their affections to shaft-driven motorcycles although completely satisfied with the "Four" in every other respect.

The brakes. Disc front and drum rear. The rear was about right and, in the dry, the disc was superb. As on so many, if not all, disc brakes it is the wet that worries us. The situation seemed to be marginally worse with the Honda than with the big Kawasaki, but perhaps that is just because we had more rain while riding the 750. The plain fact is that on

just about every disc brake that we have tried this year, British, Japanese, German and Italian, there has been a time-lag after applying the brake, in the wet, before getting results. Ride with it feathered all the time to keep the disc clear of water, some say. Ridiculous. They'll be wanting us to ride with our feet on the ground next in case we fall off. It seems to us to be an area of motorcycling that needs more work and, as things stand, makes the disc brake less of a good idea than it first appeared. Certainly this year the double-sided front disc brake, as fitted to the Morini and Benelli, has more to offer the touring rider. This is not, of course, a problem unique to Honda.

Electrically, the 750 compares well with most others in its class. The horn was pretty grim but the lights were good, the control layout was fair and the instruments were superb, especially at night. One aspect which did annoy us was the engine kill-switch mounted on top of the right hand throttle assembly. It killed the engine all right but left the starter-motor in circuit, so if one overlooked that it was in the off position, or some passing children had let curiosity get the better of them or if one's glove

inadvertently moved it (this happened to us a couple of times) the engine stopped but the starter still worked. Might we suggest that Honda look at the arrangement on the Kawasaki where the same switch kills the starter too ?

Naturally the machine comes with just about every rider aid imaginable. Stop lights activated by both front and rear brakes, twin mirrors, centre and side stands (the side stand held the machine a shade too upright), reasonable 3½-gallon petrol tank, steering lock, an array of warning lights and even a document holder, under the seat. Less attractive was a front number-plate that could be used to peel potatoes with—or slice pedestrians—and powerful ammunition for those who are campaigning to get the front number-plate abolished. As we have already indicated, we can take or leave the gold-finish on the Honda but, combined with black frame and chrome guards, it makes a pretty imposing package and, viewed overall, we would say that the bike is as handsome as they come.

It is not too difficult to criticise any bike, and when it has been around for five years, as the Honda 750 has, it is bound to have lagged behind in some areas. It has not done too badly in price, though, jumping from £680 to around £1,000 in the four-and-a-bit years since we first tried the machine. Is that too big a rise by today's standards ? We suspect not. The interesting thing is that, analysing the machine and discussing design features, there are some aspects that could be improved by riding it. That is something to be cherished. I can recall quite clearly the moment, in February 1970, when I collected a privately-owned 750 from Leytonstone and cautiously made my way across an icy London. It was a milestone in my motorcycling career. Co-incidentally the Honda that we collected from Chiswick had done almost exactly the same number of miles, about 450, as had that first one we tried. In looks it had changed hardly at all. A little more chrome here, a little less there, identical exhaust system, petrol tank, and instruments pretty much the same. Enough to give the lie to all those stories we hear that Honda change their bike every Monday morning.

The real benefit of four years development came when we rode the bike. I well recall how *civilised* I thought the first Honda that I rode was and, indeed, it was then. But standards have changed, we now take the kind of performance and equipment that Honda, almost alone, offered in 1970 for granted. With the benefit of hindsight, and using today's standards, the Honda of old seems almost crude. The present machine is very much smoother, especially from low revs., it has more torque and pulls willingly from 2,000 r.p.m., it ticks over at an even 800 r.p.m. and altogether it felt as though the past five years have been really put to good use. Performance is no longer considered the be all and end all of the Honda 750. The first bikes to arrive here made a big thing of having a top speed of 125 m.p.h. The claimed power output remains unchanged at 67 b.h.p. at 8,000 but now the bike is content to settle for not much more than 110 m.p.h. It is a much better motorcycle for it.

Perhaps the one easily-identifiable characteristic of the Honda 750 is its deep but pleasant exhaust note. That has not changed—except that it's a bit quieter now—and we can well understand how Honda owners always enjoy winding it on, just to listen to the noise. The compulsory wearing of safety helmets has removed that old saying about being able to tell an enthusiastic motorcyclist by his dirty right ear, as he rides with his head cocked listening to his engine, from the vocabulary,

but the principle still applies to the Honda owner. The Honda is still a big bike, weighing in at 503 lb with a gallon of fuel in the tank, but it sheds its weight with ease as the twistgrip is turned and the response is still as thrilling as ever. Little wonder that the bike has a reputation for wearing out chains. It is almost impossible to resist the temptation to wind it on at the slightest opportunity. That engine really is a dream, having power, flexibility and almost complete smoothness. It was not too uneconomical, either, averaging 46/49 m.p.g. during the test. If only we had been able to curb our enthusiasm it could well have been better.

Handling and comfort. They go together but are often in a different class. With the Honda they are about on a par, adequate without setting the world alight. The comfort is assisted by a 26½in-long, well-padded seat but, with a height of 33in and a wide tank to keep the legs apart, it was not perfect and stopping would be misery for a man with short legs. As it was we tended to rock from toe to toe. The footrests are also too far forward, for our taste, making the riding position more cramped than it need be. We did appreciate the handlebars, though, such a change from the sit up and beg type. They were as short as they should be while still leaving room for all the bits and pieces that have to be tacked on and were swept back to give the rider a good touring stance. Ideal for speeds up to 90 or so but uncomfortable much above. The handling has marginally improved over the years. Some of this may be due to the Bridgestone tyres, 4.00 × 18in rear, 3.25 × 19in front,

which gave us not a moment of anxiety in the wet. It would not be reasonable to say that Honda have really solved the handling problems of their biggest bike, but now its only vice is a certain choppiness when cranked over at high speed, it is gentle and not too worrying. The suspension is hard, harder than of old, and this has stiffened the machine up at the expense of more road shocks being transmitted to the rider and (more so) to a pillion passenger.

Perhaps we have become too familiar with the Honda 750 over the years; we understand it too well and know what to look for. We might also mention in passing that for the past 12,000 miles the editor's staff bike has been a Honda 750 which, although it has a hard life, has never missed a beat in all that time, has never shown the slightest sign of going off tune, starts first time, leaks a little oil, and has generally endeared itself to him. It also means that we have had longer to learn its good and bad points and, as a result, we may be more critical of the Honda than of most other bikes. On balance, though, it comes out well. It is not the cheapest of the "superbikes" but it is also a long way from being the most expensive. There are also enough of them around for the chances of finding help, in the unlikely event of it being necessary, being good. It is reasonably economical, has more than enough performance and presents it in a thrilling and, more important, useable way. Spares are not cheap but they do not seem to be much worse than any other bike in its class. In short, one of the best balanced and most reliable bikes around.

THE FIRST "BIG BIKE" IS STILL THE BEST

The CB750F2.
A report on the all-time classic of the age, in which the "Grand Old Man" proves to his numerous imitators that maturity has only served to increase its potency.

Time has proved more conclusively than any number of published analyses that, the concept was sound, the design right, the marketing strategy ably handled, the final form balanced in all respects. Almost every big motorcycle since the unveiling of the CB750 in 1969 has paid it homage by imitation, and the Honda 750 Four, even now, provides the standard by which motorcyclists the world over judge their motorcycles.

When it hit the roads nothing compared to it as an exciting, functional, sporting roadster, although contempories occasionally matched, even beat individual ancillary performances. Nothing, though, offered quite the same generous bulk of all-encompassing modern motorcycling.

Then came Kawa's "Big Mutha" Z fours, Suzuki's Kettle, Yamaha's XS750 twin, of which only the former has survived as an on-going model, probably because it adopted the same stance as Honda's four stroke, transverse four. Now there's a slightly smaller Kawasaki, the Z650, and a Suzuki GS750, and even Yamaha have accepted the seemingly inevitable with their new XS 750 triple. One by one the new bikes are welcomed into the market, each one boasting of some special, unique feature intended to place it at the top of the pile.

THE FIRST "BIG BIKE"

Each year sees what is presumed by many to be the last of the founder member of the modern big motorcycle, yet each year it matches its challengers. This year, the Grand Old Man of them all has undergone such drastic monkey gland treatment as to make the difference between its two variations — CB750K and CB750F2, quite startling.

Styling is unchanged from the CB750F1, although a new paint job lends the model an improved appearance, but the performance is much sharper, making it one of the two fastest 750's on sale today. The other one? That's another story altogether.

A brand new head gives better breathing and new cams and timing push the gas through quicker. A new exhaust system looks after the increase in power - as does the much modified clutch.

To Honda's credit, they have treated the revisioning of their cruiserweight sportster as a total package so, although the engine has been uprated, the rest of the machine's components have followed suit. The result is not simply a more powerful engine, but a faster, safer motorcycle. To give an example of this let me tell you about the time when the new Hondas were launched to the press.

I was cruising comfortably at my favourite speed, relaxed, enjoying the F2's improved ride, having time enough to study various aspects of its performance. We came to a junction 40 miles along the road, where I stopped to await the others coming along on smaller motorcycles behind. After perhaps three minutes, Mike Scott, Features Editor of Superbike, arrived on his 750K, all red-faced and gasping. "Jeez. It was you, was it? I've been trying to keep you in sight on this (pointing to the 750K) but I couldn't." Now then, whatever you might like to think about motorcycles journalists, some of whom are simply sports reporters who occasionally, and disastrously, ride and write about motorcycles, others, such as Scott, are fine, fast riders. The significant thing here is that I was swinging through the countryside without effort, and unpressurised. Scott, who is at least my equal as far as fast riding goes, was unable to hold, let alone catch me from the saddle of the touring K, and when Scott tries, Scott tries.

Inside the engine of the F2 much is different. The head is a brand new one, with inlet tracts enlarged from 30 to 32mm, and inlet valves upped from 32 to 34mm. This makes the most of the new 28mm Keihin carburettors, which now sport accelerator pumps and eliminate the flat spots that once troubled some 750 Fours. Combustion chamber shape is unchanged from last year but compression is nominally lowered from 9.2:1 to 9:1 in order that cheap petrol might be better utilised. Fiercer valve timing has been employed and the new cam also lifts the valves half a millimetre more. To pass the extra gas sucked into the engine by these modifications the exhaust valves have been increased in size from 28 to 31mm, and a new exhaust system with larger capacity silencer, of improved silencing efficiency also, completes the power train changes.

One thing leads to another, as any home tuner knows only too well, and Honda engineers have taken everything into account by modifying the clutch so that it might cope with the extra power, now up to 72 bhp. Incidentally, Honda measure all power from the crankshaft under DIN regulations, which means they take no account of power loss through the transmission, but figures are proven under the rigorous conditions imposed by DIN regulations. Springs of increased strength were fitted to the clutch, but the lift mechanism altered so that no greater handlebar leverage is required to operate it. The plates are now eased further apart during de-clutching, a modification which Honda claim has eliminated the odd rattles issuing from some older models during idling with the clutch plates lifted.

There is a new bottom end too. The crankshaft is stronger, and now runs in what amount to Vandervell type thin wall plain bearings of a bronze/lead/tin alloy, rather than the old aluminium type. More strength has been inbuilt by the adoption of stronger head studs, and the barrell itself is heavier, therefore stronger, than previously.

THE FIRST "BIG BIKE"

Suspension is much improved by new, firmer damping in both tele-forks and pivoted fork units, and the spring rating has also been slightly increased to match.

Braking has been equally well tended. Twin discs are fitted as standard on the front wheel, and one on the rear. The calipers are of the fully floating type, moving along a stainless steel pin as required during braking, and the master cylinder is larger, and of a remote type away from the lever on the handlebar.

Wheels are of the now standard Honda alloy rim and hub joined by pressed steel spokes riveted and bolted into place.

Right from the time the starter button is pressed (kick starting being retained for those of us who feel a bike ain't a bike without a grudge-buffer) it is apparent

The illustration below shows the new 28mm Keihin carburettors with accelerator pumps to eliminate those flat spots.

something is different because the engine responds to the twistgrip more quickly than any Honda yet, and when you sit on it it feels tight, right. The impression grows as the ride progresses, especially out on hte open road, although there is no reason to assume that it is the F2's only happy hunting grounds. Drifting gently and quietly through town is as regular as you could wish for, but lacking the soft plush ease of the 750K, obviously, so we'll skip the town stuff and get out into the country.

What with one thing and another the thing feels compact, ready to move, probably as much concerned with the new riding position, arranged, as is Honda's new fashion, to promote compatability between the man and his machine. In this case a set of semi-flat and short handlebar bends, and repositioned footrests, back perhaps an inch on their new cast aluminium mountings from the F1, afford an ideal compromise between boulevard cruiser and cafe-racer. I was reminded of the old style British twins when they were built by motorcyclists who rode their products. Say what you like, the key to good riding lies completely with the rider's position because if he is right, then weight distribution is good and handling is easy and stability top-notch.

Admittedly you can sit down all soft and squodgy "inside" a 750K and feel luxuriously cossetted but, as Mike Scott discovered, there's more to fast riding than pandering to soft rumps. The rider has to be laid so he can cruise fast without hanging on to the handlebars, for instance. If you know how a CB400F feels, then you will appreciate the very similar F2 as its behaviour and stance at speed.

The acceleration of the machine through its gears was incredibly fast. Over a standing quarter I managed a best time of 13.1 seconds after just two preliminaries, by which time the speed was 102 mph. Given

more practice sessions doubtless it would have been faster still. Top speed achieved in a bulky stormsuit over leathers was 115 mph, with yours truly crouching into the wind, but not prone. We had no chance for anything else because of the filthy weather blanketing the entire test period, but as maximum power is developed at 9000 rpm now, 500 up on the F1, and the bike was achieving 115 mph regularly on only 7000 rpm, there is little doubt that someone lighter than my 200 lbs (in full bike clothing) wearing racing, or even touring, leathers would improve on both acceleration and top speed. If these things are not managing 120, even 125 mph once fully run in I'll be very surprised indeed.

Best of it is that stability is excellent even over 100 mph. There was nothing wrong with the F1 in but the improved F2 Show a damping and extra inch on the wheelbase has uprated the chassis performance even more. Once or twice when reversing power during high speed curving approaches to hazards some way ahead the machine did waver a little, but it was mild and not particularly disturbing. When I commented on this to a well-known Honda dealer and tuner he commented that it was due to the immensely heavy (30 lbs he said) silencer along one side of the bike. He has redistributed the weight by using a special Japanese made exhaust system but, as this is admittedly noisier, I think I would prefer the mild and harmless shimmies at speed to the loss of the F2's otherwise highly commendable silence. This way it can be used fast without attracting attention.

Vibration there was none, although the firm suspension and more powerful engine could fool you into believing it was a coarser motorcycle. By the 750K's standards it probably is, but you can't have it all ways. Nevertheless, it was possible to murmer through town at under 2000 rpm on a gentle fist. I managed 27 mph 1850 rpm, and still accelerated away without any signs of machine protest.

Fast cornering was excellent, although hampered slightly by the fat silencer on the right side. On a flat road this would be no problem, but as we ride on the left in Britain it ensures that, combined with the adverse camber of most roads, right handers did foul up the otherwise fine line. The thing is a little higher than it was, and only scrapes when pushed hard, or with a pillion rider, but considering the price of the thing will probably be around £40 or more, damaging it for the average bend swinger could cause financial problems.

Fuel consumption is down on what it once was, even allowing for the higher speeds encouraged. Flat out A type road riding resulted in an overall average of exactly 30 mpg. The cruising average proved to be exactly 40 mpg, strangely enough. Speed extracts its own penalties, however. Power needs fuelling.

The rest of the machine was all solid Honda, meaning it was meat and potato pie right through, all familiar, all trustworthy, all durable, all reliable. It's nice to have all that, and a bit of kick as well. Suzuki GS 750's look to your new laurels.

OWNER'S VIEW

To discover the advantages and drawbacks of running the CB750 models I sought the opinion of Eric Warburton and Dave Ayesthorpe. Eric specialises in the early CB750 and has aquired an almost encyclopaedic knowledge of the range as a by-product of the exhaustive research necessary for his restoration work. Dave, on the other hand, has built up a formidable collection of early Honda models, and as such has formed a detailed but more objective view of the CB750. The two opinions in the following pages should give the prospective owner a good idea of what to expect from the 750.

PS: Why are you interested in the Honda CB750?

EW: When the CB750 was launched it had such an impact that you had to take notice. Modern bikes may be more sophisticated and laden with gimmicks, but the CB750 would still hold its own in all respects with most modern bikes.

DA: My current interest is because the CB750 was an important milestone in Honda history, and therefore forms an essential part of my Honda collection.

PS: When and why did you buy your Honda CB750?

EW: After owning my first CB750, a 1971 model which I purchased in 1974, I decided that one day I would rebuild an older model to original specification. I sold my first machine in 1975 and started to look for an older bike, which I finally located in St Albans, Herts. This was purchased in February 1977, more for its age than condition.

DA: The original CB750 was bought in 1971 as a logical improvement on the CB450 that was in use until that time.

PS: What condition was it in? If you found faults, were these common problems on the CB750?

EW: As I mentioned before, it was purchased for its age rather than condition, and it had the faults common at that time to all early CB750s. These were mainly that owners would replace tanks, side panels, headlamp shrouds and shell, clocks, exhausts and seat with those of the later models. These fitted but were of a different style and colour. Mine had been changed in this way but was otherwise in fairly good condition.

DA: Condition was almost as new. No faults were found other than the standard handlebars which were too high. These were changed for CB250 bars initially, clip-ons being fitted later. Later problems were rotting exhausts, an apparently new problem at the time, but later a common fault due to the cooler running of the four-pipe system. Other common problems which eventually manifested themselves were final drive shaft bearing failure, modified on later models, and a tendency for the final drive chain to snap and smash the crankcase if excessively worn. The swinging arm bushes were subject to somewhat rapid wear.

PS: What repair or renovation work has been done? Is there a better way of tackling the problems, and what advice would you give someone facing the same problems? Would it have been an economic proposition to have bought a machine in better or worse condition than yours originally?

EW: The bike has been totally rebuilt from the wheels upwards. The renovation on the original parts was fairly straightforward – replating, polishing and spraying. The problems started when I wanted exact original appearance, and a lot of money was wasted trying to match paintwork, for example. After having all the coloured parts sprayed using photographs and one new side panel as a colour match, I eventually traced new parts which were slightly different. I have spent nearly £3000 getting the bike back to original specification, and it has taken me five years. I could have purchased a more original machine, but it would have been a later model. Given that I wanted the earliest possible example I think that I have ended up with a fair compromise. To someone facing the same task I would advise them to buy new parts to preserve originality, but not to bother unless they are prepared to devote a lot of money and time to the project.

DA: I replaced the final drive shaft bearings after failure at about 30,000 miles, and again when all the other gearbox bearings were replaced at about 60,000. Worn piston rings were renewed at 45,000 miles, but the engine did not need reboring. The cam chain and primary chains were renewed as a matter of course at the same time. The big end and main bearings, bores, pistons, valves and, unusually, the contact breakers are all original at 78,000 miles.

The machine was of optimum value when purchased one year old with 3,000 miles on the clock.

PS: Have you experienced difficulty in obtaining any parts? What solutions did you find?

EW: Even if you are prepared to devote time and money on restoration there is another problem. This is knowing what is an original part and what isn't. I have wasted a lot of money sending for parts from all over the country only to discover when they arrive that they are K2 or K6 parts. Buying the manufacturer's service literature and parts books, and visiting shops in person is the only way of ensuring that you get the correct part. Even some of the main Honda dealers think that the first 750 Honda was the K1.

DA: My only problem was obtaining the new gearbox mainshaft bearing, probably due to lack of demand for this part. A standard bearing of the correct dimensions was purchased and the locating groove then ground in the outer race.

PS: What kind of performance and handling does the machine have?

EW: There has been a lot of talk over the years about the 'ill-handling' CB750, but people forget that it is basically a touring bike – not a lane scratching bike. If set up properly and well maintained the bike will handle well within the capabilities of most tourers. If you want to go chasing round the lanes the power will overwhelm the handling if you're not careful. Performance is what got the CB750 noticed in 1969/70, various tests quoting top speeds of 125 mph and a standing quarter of just over 12 seconds. I have found on all three of the CB750s owned that this is possible as long as the bike is in top tune and well serviced. Given that the bike was launched fourteen years ago modern equivalents do not offer much more power, unless of bigger capacity.

DA: Performance is good but has obviously been left behind by the latest generation of bikes. Handling is good two-up, but poor when ridden solo.

PS: Is your machine in regular use? How practical is it? Are the running costs high?

EW: My CB750 is not in regular use because I have started to enter it in concours events and obviously have to keep it in top condition which you can't do if riding it in all weathers. My CB750K0 is in regular use, but mostly during the summer. The running costs are not high by modern standards, the main expense being on oil and filters, though rear tyres and chains won't last long if you are heavy on

the throttle. Fuel consumption again depends on throttle use, varying between 35 and 50 mpg.

DA: The machine was in regular use until 1977 and is now in semi-retirement. It is now used mainly for an annual trip to the Isle of Man for the TT. It is only really practical for long distance work, at which it excels, apart from the chain final drive. Running costs are reasonable given its size and performance.

PS: Has your machine won any prizes in concours or similar events?

EW: Yes. 3rd place at the Honda day at Donington in July 1979. Best Japanese at the Classic Bike Show, Belle Vue in October 1982. Best Modern at the Bristol Classic Bike Show in February 1983. The bike has also been featured in *Classic Bike, Hondaway* and *Which Bike?* I would like to enter more competitions, but do not have the spare time at present.

PS: Are there any owners clubs or clubs which cater specially for Hondas; if so, how helpful is it to be a member?

EW: I would recommend being a member of the Vintage Japanese Owners Club. A lot of information and literature from all over the world can be traced through the club. The Honda Owners Club is specifically for Honda owners, but modern bikes tend to be the main topic of conversation.

DA: The Honda Owners Club which was established in 1961. Help is forthcoming if you are prepared to put yourself out to find it – as it is in most clubs. The Vintage Japanese Owners Club can be of help to owners of the early models.

PS: Is there a specialist whom you have found to be particularly helpful?

EW: A lot of people have helped over the past seven years. The list could be endless, but the people who have been particularly helpful are:

    Hadleigh Custom (when they dealt with Honda parts).

    Bill Smith Motorcycles,

Cheshire.

    P.F.K. Lings, Norfolk.

DA: Yes – Bill Smith Motorcycles, Cheshire.

PS: How much enjoyment do you get from your machine?

EW: I get a lot of enjoyment, not only from owing a CB750, but also as a hobby. I have built up a collection of parts and literature and this is increasing all the time. The bike is now recognised as a classic and is always an attraction at shows. This gives me a lot of enjoyment and makes it all worthwhile.

DA: How do you quantify enjoyment? The fact that I prefer to take the CB750 to the Isle of Man each year rather than the Gold Wing which I usually ride probably speaks for itself. The bike would not have covered 75,000 miles, mostly with my wife and myself aboard, if we hadn't enjoyed it.

PS: What advice would you give to potential 750 owners?

EW: I would advise them to think very carefully about their choice. You could buy a K2 or K6 for a fraction of the money I have spent, or you could spend a great deal of time and money putting together an early model. The parts are getting harder to trace for an original model, but for me part of the enjoyment is in searching and research.

DA: The same as to any other Honda owner – keep the oil and filter changed regularly!! Two-stroke oil down the exhausts **may** stop them rotting.

The benefit of experience

During the long and often frustrating search for original parts, Eric Warburton has become something of a guru of the early 750. The resulting detailed knowledge of the model is of inestimable value to any would-be restorer, and has been reproduced below from a set of notes which

Eric sent me when I was compiling this book.

**Changes: Model to model :-
Changes on CB750
Engine No to 1044847
Frame No to 1044825**

There were many minor changes on this model to parts such as crankcases. These were changed three times with changes on bearing set rings, bolt lengths, numbers of bolts, seals, oil filter housing which was finned very early on. Only four valve guide seals were fitted to No 1014966, from then onwards eight were fitted. The clutch was also changed very early ie outer, outer ring, main plate, wire stopper ring, springs, spring seats. A chain guide under the sprocket cover was used only on Numbers 1026144-1044805. The gearbox selectors were changed early ie. two bolts and associated parts used up to Number 1026143 including double tab washer. After this one bolt, one stud and no tab washer were used. Also assembly on end of gear shift drum changed accordingly. No significant changes of appearance occurred. Colours: Candy Blue Green or Candy Ruby Red.

**Changes on CB750K0.
Engine No 1044848-1045147
Frame No 1044826-1044947**

This version of the 750 Four appeared during the transitional period from CB750 to CB750K1. The machine embodies only some of the CB750K1 modifications, and in all only 36 units were sold in the UK. Again there were a lot of minor changes, the most significant being to the carburetters. These were changed to the 'bar lift' type incorporating only two cables not four, the handlebar control was also changed. A black ribbed filter box was fitted as opposed to the previous flat, coloured box; this was done to prevent cracking. Other minor changes as follows:- an adjustable chain oiler was fitted in

the centre of the engine sprocket, which was changed from 16T to 18T. The rear sprocket was also changed from 45T to 48T. The engine sprocket cover was altered in shape to clear the bigger sprocket. The fork legs use bigger seals and retaining circlips and the rear suspension was increased in diameter. The front wheel hub was 4 mm narrower and all the disc mounting bolts shortened to suit. The front brake lever adjuster was changed from a half round stud and nut to a rubber and flat retaining plate. The ignition switch was changed from a recessed front to a flat front with the plastic boss removed from the key to suit. This is a change I could not understand as the original recessed switch is more watertight than the later one. The shape of the rear wheel cush drive rubbers was changed along with the sprockets to try and increase chain life. Colours were as the CB750.

**Changes on CB750K1.
Engine No 1045148-2000000
Frame No 1044948-2000000**

This is when major changes were made which to me is when Honda started to try and tone down the size of the machine and in my opinion ruined the looks. The side panels were changed to a more rounded shape with new badges. A new oil tank also had to be fitted. The seat was flattened and narrowed at the front. The clocks were altered to a flat black face with glass covers instead of acrylic resin, which was affected by brake fluid. Again minor changes were made to the engine, much the same as previously mentioned. A new colour scheme was introduced, this being Candy Gold (CQ) and the

Candy Blue Green was dropped.

**Changes on CB750K2.
Engine No 2000000 onwards
Frame No 2000000 onwards**

Again major changes took place on this model and it looked nothing like the original CB750. The engine was detuned and noticeably slower. New exhaust pipes had different baffles. New clocks had no warning lights in them. These latter were fitted in a panel which replaced the handlebar clamps. Flat bars were fitted. A black headlamp shell with chrome shrouds and large reflectors replaced the coloured ones with small reflectors. A new petrol tank was used, finished in Candy Gold Custom (LX) and with white badges. A new style seat and lock was also fitted. The rear light unit was changed and the front mudguard no longer needed a front number plate so this was changed too. The front brake caliper was painted black in place of silver. The list of minor changes is endless but the overall appearance changed drastically.

The changes continued on models K3, 4, 5, but the next model for the UK was the K6. Again this was changed but only in minor respects. In comparison, the CB750, K0 and K1 were all similar whilst the CB750K2, K3, K4, K5 and K6 were all similar to one another but drastically different from the earlier models.

BUYING

Which model?

Finding a used CB750 should present the prospective purchaser with few problems, and in most instances the price should be reasonable. It is unlikely that an original model CB750 or the transitional CB750 K0 will be found — most were scrapped long ago and any that remain are beginning to be of interest to collectors. If you **do** decide to go for an early model, remember that spares for the pre-K1 type can be quite difficult to obtain and in many instances availability will depend entirely on how good the local storeman is, and how extensive is his stock of early parts.

It is perfectly possible to place an order for an obscure early part with Honda, via a reputable Honda dealer, but this often results in a later part being sent. This is because the parts system is computerised, and usually updates original part numbers to the latest version. If you are determined to attempt a full restoration, do not be fooled into thinking that, being a modern machine, it will be easy — it will probably prove harder in some areas than restoring a post-war British machine. For those who intend to persevere, you have Eric Warburton's machine as inspiration

and proof that it can be done, at a cost.

The later 'K' models are likely to be the most commonly available. Identifying a specific model may prove difficult unless the engine and frame numbers are checked carefully. It is unlikely that the machine will be in original condition, and most will have non-standard tyres, rear suspension units and possibly exhaust systems fitted. This should not discourage purchase — most owners will have modified the above to save money and improve performance.

The F1 and F2 versions were the sporty models of the range and may well reflect a harder life, and this in turn will require careful checking for expensive engine noises and obviously worn final drive components.

It has often been said of the CB750 range that the earlier models were faster. This is borne out to some extent by contemporary road test performance figures which reflected the gradual drop in performance as noise and gas emission laws were tightened. What should be borne in mind is that road test figures are really of academic rather than practical interest, and that the average K6 will be in better general condition than a similarly used K2.

Taken overall, the best practical proposition would be a late K model — K6 or K7 or possibly the sportier F2 version.

'It's all right, sir, they all do that ...'

If you mention just about any machine to a group of motorcyclists you can guarantee that it will provoke a pretty horrifying account of its 'weak points'. A few of these will be valid criticisms, a few more will be true as far as one particular machine is concerned but the majority will be part of the folklore

that seems to abound in motorcycling.

Equally, the prospective seller, be he a salesman or private individual will no doubt be anxious to reassure you about the expensive sounding clatter that is emanating from the bowels of the engine. The truth of the matter lies somewhere between the two extremes, so if at all possible, get someone who *really* knows the model to check it over for you before you buy, and don't be put off by too many horror stories.

The CB750 is, by modern standards a rather crude machine, and is inclined to be mechanically noisy if compare with a modern equivalent. It is also very tough, however, and as such represents a good buy, even after a fairly high mileage has been recorded. It is unusual for the engine to require much attention before 50,000 miles, and in practice it is quite common for twice this mileage or more to be covered before an engine overhaul is required. The chassis is best described as adequate in its standard form, but it can be improved upon without great expenditure.

The engine and transmission

The engine castings will probably look quite shabby — they are difficult to keep clean, particularly once the engine lacquer has begun to flake off. Oil leaks are unusual on all but the very early machines, where a gradual seepage at the cylinder head joint was not uncommon. Do not worry about a lot of oil around the gearbox sprocket. This is usually caused by an over-enthusiastic chain oiler and can be adjusted.

Check for unusual engine noise once the engine has reached normal temperature — if possible after taking the machine for a test ride. At idle speed clutch chatter is quite common, and can usually be traced to bad carburettor synchronisation. There were a number of modifications which reduced this, but the real answer is to get the carburettors balanced. The clutch noise is itself annoying but not likely to foretell serious problems. The noise tends to go away above idle speed, and most owners learn to ignore it. The clutch itself is very tough and should not give much trouble. It does tend to be a bit sudden in action, but this ceases to be obtrusive once its action is familiar.

The primary drive chain, on all but the CB750 A, is of the roller type rather than the Morse or Hy-Vo type now used almost exclusively. Legend has it that the chains are prone to breakage or wear unevenly (they run as a pair on duplex sprockets) but there is little evidence that they do so more than any other engine. The chains should last between engine overhauls *unless the oil level has run low* in the past.

Cam chains have also been accused of being a weak point in the engine, and again I have found little real evidence that this is so. What can happen, again due to failed lubrication, is that the tensioner rollers may overheat and break up, with fairly serious engine damage to follow, if the tensioner is not renewed promptly. The tensioner can be inspected with the engine in the frame, but a top-end overhaul will be necessary to renew it, involving engine removal.

The gearbox is about as indestructible as the clutch, and unlikely to cause problems. There were selection problems on the very first machines, but these were cured by the introduction of a much improved selector mechanism with far better indexing and a solid positive stop arrangement to prevent over-selection. The modification was made after the 450th machine off the production line – so selection problems are very unlikely. It is just possible that a badly abused machine may jump out of gear, and if so this will

usually be caused by worn engagement dogs. The problem can be cured by fitting new gears, but again this will require a full engine strip.

A more common source of trouble is the bearing nearest the sprocket on the output shaft. This was originally located by a groove in the bearing outer race which engaged a half-ring in the crankcase boss. This arrangement caused unforeseen problems if the final drive chain was over-tightened – the bearing broke up causing extensive damage to the gearbox and crankcases. To avoid the weak area, the bearing groove was omitted, the new bearing being located by a flat circlip outboard of the bearing. Later still, from about the K6 model, a revised double bearing was used to reinforce the shaft area still further. The moral of this saga is to check that the bearing is sound when purchasing by removing the sprocket cover and feeling for play in the shaft (take care not to mistake the normal free movement of the sprocket) and to avoid overtightening the chain.

There have been tales of camshaft problems in the past, mostly concerning the camshaft seizing in its bearing surfaces. This is almost invariably caused by oil starvation due to the small oil restrictor nozzles below the cylinder head face becoming obstructed. There are usually two reasons for this, the main one being the use of poor quality pattern oil filters. These can allow enough debris to pass through and into the cylinder head oil feed to block the restrictors and cause lubrication failure. To be safe, always use genuine Honda oil filters. The second cause is failure to clean out all oilways during an overhaul, thus creating the same problem. On very early engines, the restrictors are a press fit in the casting and should be cleaned with a solvent and blown through with compressed air. Later models have easily removable items which should be taken out and cleaned. Above all, make absolutely sure of

clinical cleanliness during assembly.

The chassis

Apart from the normal checks on steering, suspension, brakes, electrical system and general condition there are a few areas which should be looked at more closely on the CB750 range.

Firstly, have a good look at the exhaust system, especially on the 'K' models with their expensive and rust-prone four-into-four system. The silencers, like most silencers, rot through from the inside with the assistance of acidic exhaust gases, particularly when the small drain holes at the lowest point of the system become blocked. If any rust holes are evident, add the cost of a new system to the asking price. It is very likely that you will find a 'K' model fitted with the four-into-one 'F' type exhaust system, or a similar after market job. These are far less prone to rusting because they run much hotter. They are also considerably cheaper and a lot lighter, so unless you are determined to have the four original silencers for originality, stick to the four-into-one arrangement. If fitting such a system to replace the four pipe set, remember to check carburettor jetting which may need altering to suit. A reputable exhaust system manufacturer will be able to advise on the likely changes. If he can't, go elsewhere because ignorance on this point may indicate that the proposed system has not been tested properly.

The frame itself has two genuinely weak points; the swinging arm bushes and the steering head races. Check the swinging arm for free play by pushing it from side to side. If you feel movement in the bushes, they need renewing. The original plastic bushes are acceptable when in good condition, but no more than that. Far better are the phosphor bronze items available from a number of Honda specialists. They are not genuine parts, but they should improve handling a great deal. On the same subject, it is worth dismantling, cleaning and re-greasing the pivot once a year rather than rely on the grease nipples getting the grease to where it's needed. This is particularly true of the early arrangement with a nipple at each end of the pivot.

The problem with the steering head bearings is simply that they were too weak for the application and tended to indent the races rather quickly. This can often be felt if the wheel is raised clear of the ground and the steering turned from lock to lock. Any notchiness means that the bearings are worn out. If new bearings are to be fitted, try to obtain a taper roller conversion. This arrangement will last almost indefinitely, and will transform the steering, making the machine feel much tauter on the road. The bearing conversion kits are widely available from mail order suppliers, and like most accessories and tuning parts may be found through advertisements in the motorcycle press.

CLUBS, SPECIALISTS & BOOKS

Clubs

Now that the sohc 750 is an obsolete model it is less easy to come by detailed knowledge from dealers, and parts for the early versions are getting more and more difficult to acquire. It is very useful, if not essential, to have some sort of help especially when the model is unfamiliar. Owners Clubs provide a pool of knowledge that will prove invaluable. Talking to other owners will provide the necessary contacts for obscure parts, and may often produce the parts themselves.

Enthusiasts and restorers should join the Vintage Japanese Motorcycle Club, who have the specialist knowledge, relating to the early versions, necessary to steer a rebuild through to completion. The Honda Owners Club will be of interest to less committed owners and to owners of the later models.

Honda Owners Club
UK Contact:
Dave Barton,
18 Embley Close,
Calmore,
Southampton.

Vintage Japanese Motorcycle Club
UK Contact:
Colin Gibson (Hon. Sec.),
326 Ashley Down Road,
Bristol BS7 9BQ.

US Contact:
Barton Taylor,
301 Phelps Avenue,
Bergenfield,
New Jersey,
07621.
USA.

Australian Contact:
Mick Godfrey,
P.O. Box 270,
Elizabeth,
S.A. 5112,
Australia.

Specialists

The sohc CB750 is in the rather grey transitional area between being an 'old bike' and a classic, thus there are no firms specialising in these models alone. It is possible, however, to get almost any part for any model, given time, from any good Honda dealer. When discussing this with owners, the unanimous opinion is that it is vital to find an enthusiastic and dedicated storeman, who will be prepared to take the extra trouble required to get the original parts rather than later parts which will fit but may be of different design. This means side-stepping Honda's parts computer system in some instances. Shop around the local dealers, and stick with the one who seems most enthusiastic.

There follows the names and addresses of a few of the suppliers that have proved helpful to 750 owners in the past:

Rex Judd,
415 Burnt Oak,
Broadway,
Edgware,
Middlesex.

Fowlers of Bristol Ltd,
2-12 Bath Road,
Bristol BS4 3DR.

John Skellern Ltd,
23-25 and 34-36 Friar St,
Worcester WR1 2NA.

Tommy Robb and
Bill Smith Ltd,
240 Manchester Rd,
Warrington,
Chesire WA1 3BE.

P.F.K. Ling Ltd,
Redenhall Road,
Harleston,
Norfolk.

Books

To the best of my knowledge, this is the only book currently in print which relates solely to the sohc Honda CB750S. If, as is likely, the models become more widely accepted as classics of their era, there will no doubt follow a definitive work on the subject in the years to come. In the meantime, the following reference list should prove of interest to owners and restorers.

Honda 750 Four Owners Workshop Manual by Jeff Clew, book number 131. Published in 1974 by the Haynes Publishing Group, and revised in 1980, this book covers all of the sohc 750s, including the automatic CB750A model. This should provide a good deal of practical information for the enthusiast restorer and casual rider alike, and is a sound alternative to Honda's own excellent but expensive service manuals.

The Story of Honda Motorcycles by Peter Carrick. Published in 1976 by Patrick Stephens Ltd.

A general history of the Honda company, the book charts the growth of Honda during the 1960s and 1970s, with emphasis on the competition successes during that period. It contains a number of references to the CB750, mostly relating to the early days of the model and the impact that it had when launched alongside the then current large capacity twins.

Japanese Motorcycles by Cyril Ayton. Published in 1982 by the Hamlyn Publishing Group.

Japanese Motorcycles: the machines and the men behind them by Cyril Ayton. Published in 1981 by Frederick Muller Ltd.

The above titles cover roughly similar ground, and should be of general interest to all Honda owners.

PHOTO GALLERY

1. Right-hand view of the original model CB750, this restored example belonging to Eric Warburton. In terms of general design it is worth noting how little the machine changed in its production life, though there were numerous detail changes.

2. A left-hand view of the same machine, and useful reference for any would-be restorer. It is interesting that certain features, like the fqur-pipe exhaust system with heat shields on the upper silencers, remained a constant part of the K series.

3

4

5

3. Viewed from the rear, the CB750 seems surprisingly slim for a four, though by modern standards the engine is wide across the crankcase area. The originality of this machine even extends to the tyres – these are the original-pattern Bridgestones.

4. In this shot, the front fork gaiters, which remained a standard feature for many years, can be seen. Also visible is the ribbed front tyre. Some of the CB750's handling problems may have resulted from the fitting of block pattern front tyres which could sometimes induce a wobble at speed.

5. At the same time of its launch, the heavily-finned engine was reckoned to be impossible to keep clean, and thousands of shabby CB750 variants have reinforced this view over the years. This engine is fourteen years old – draw your own conclusions.

6. The front forks were adequate in operation and very well protected from the elements. Note that the fork shrouds and integral headlamp brackets were painted to match the fuel tank and side panels. The front mudguard design was changed on UK models when the requirement for a pedestrian-slicing front number plate was dropped.

7. The four-pipe exhaust system was hardly understated, but soon attracted a following of its own. The system runs very cool but is prone to rotting, even when looked after. Replacement systems are not cheap. Heat shield protects passenger's feet from the hot silencer and the hot silencer from melted shoe soles.

8. Pillion footrest mounting runs between the two silencers. Note that one of the two swinging arm grease nipples is visible in this shot – replaced by a single central item on later versions.

9. Handlebar control and instrument layout was neat and uncluttered with all warning lamps incorporated in instrument faces. Single throttle cable denotes the all-cable system used on the CB750 model only. Fuel filler cap is of the quick release, or 'Monza', type.

10. Centre and prop stands were supplied as standard equipment, both being of fairly robust construction and functional in use.

6

7

8

9

10

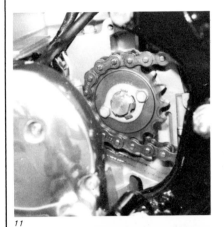

11

12

13

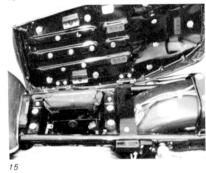

14

15

11.   Early models were equipped with a non-adjustable final drive chain oiler which lubricated the chain with engine oil via the gearbox output shaft. Compare this with photograph 31 which shows the later, adjustable variety.

12.   Many of the electrical components are housed behind the left-hand side panel. All are easily accessible and in most cases can be unplugged from the loom. In the foreground is the small and rather rudimentary fuse box, which was made more comprehensive on later versions.

13.   Clearly visible in this shot is the painted air cleaner casing, again peculiar to the CB750 model and a reliable identifying feature. Also visible are the direct cable runs to the carburettor, also modified on KO and subsequent models.

14.   The hydraulic front disc brake was a recent innovation on production machines when the CB750 emerged. Later versions had a black caliper of this design, whilst the F2 had a completely revised braking system.

15.   With the hinged dualseat lifted, the (empty) battery compartment can be seen. Behind it is a recess which contains the tool roll. Access to both is simple in the extreme.

16

17

18

19

16.   The unusual view of the right-hand handlebar end shows the brake master cylinder assembly. Brake lever stop adjuster was omitted on later models – US product liability laws strike again!

17.   This side view shows most of the distinguishing features of the original CB750 model; side panel, air cleaner and carburettors. Note also the ignition switch location which remained on all of the earlier versions.

18.   Eric Warburton astride his masterpiece. The fact that he is still smiling after all the time, money and hard work that this machine has cost him says much of his tenacity during the project. He now owns a machine which is unique and of which he is justifiably proud.

19.   Jeff Clew, who edited this book, is better known as a British bike enthusiast and author. This didn't stop his sampling what the opposition had to offer. The bike is **probably** a CB750 which was registered late, and seems to have lost its side panel badges.

20.   This shot shows details of footrest and brake pedal locations and folding kickstart arrangement. Note also the heavy reinforced oil tank lines and the swinging arm pivot grease nipple.

20

21

22

23

24

25

21. Close-up of rear hub and sprocket mounting on CB750. This was modified on K0 and later models – compare this photograph with 22 to spot the differences.

22. Same view of rear hub as in 21 above, but this time of CB750K0 model. Differences are minor, but can cause problems when ordering spares.

23. The left-hand switch assembly – CB750 type.

24. The right-hand switch assembly – CB750 type.

25. This was the original ignition switch location, and it was retained for some years on the K series models, through the exact design varied over the years. Some loved the arrangement and some hated it, but at least your keys didn't ruin the instrument panel.

26. Compare this view of the CB750K0 with the shot of the CB750 in photograph 1, and there are few obvious differences. Closer examination reveals this not to be the case, as we shall see.

26

27

28

29

30

27. Another angle on the CB750K0. Rear suspension units were of gas-filled De Carbon pattern. Quite advanced at the time, but they never proved popular and were almost invariably uprated.

28. Very few clues in this photograph which would differentiate between the K0 and the CB750. Compare with photograph 6.

29. A right-hand view of the K0 engine unit reveals few differences unless you look closely. Engine crashbars are non-standard, but worthwhile.

30. Seen from the left-hand side the oil filter housing is clearly visible between the centre pipes. The central retaining bolts were commonly overtightened and can often be found with sockets welded permanently to them to facilitate removal. This is unnecessary if you know what you are doing.

31. Look closer and the changes become evident. This shot shows the chain oiler adjuster and locknut. Compare this with photograph 11.

31

32

33

32.   A clear illustration of the new air cleaner casing fitted to the K0 and later models. Compare this with the painted type shown in photograph 13.

33.   The underseat area of the K0 showing the battery and toolkit. This is identical to the CB750 layout shown in photograph 15.

34.   Note the short stub connecting the two silencers, an arrangement common to the four-pipe 'K' models.

35.   A detail shot of the K0 engine unit showing the same features as depicted in photograph 20. No changes here.

36.   A general view of the K0, the transition model that almost never existed. It is important because it embodies many of the original revisions to the CB750.

34

35

36

37

38

39

41

40

42

43

37. This could be a shot of a CB750 except for the two throttle cables which indicate a K0 model. The two cables open and close the bar linkage throttle assembly that replaced the four cables.

38. With the tank and seat removed, the four separate throttle cables can be seen clearly on this CB750. The arrangement worked less than perfectly, requiring frequent synchronisation to maintain even running.

39. Viewed from above, the rubber-gaitered operating links on the K0 carburettors can be seen. This system was a great improvement on the original type.

40. Another view of the bar linkage arrangement in which the operating pulley and the push-pull throttle cables can be seen. Compare this shot with 38.

41. This side panel design and the Honda wing emblem was use on the CB750 and K0. In this case it is the latter model, identifiable by the fluted air cleaner casing.

42. Dave Ayesthorpe's Honda CB750 Automatic, a machine never offered for sale in the UK, though

reasonable numbers were sold in the US. Note how the styling has been changed to emphasise its touring role. Plastic deflector to the rear of the brake caliper is to improve wet weather braking performance.

43. Seen from the right, the 'F' type exhaust system is evident, as is the large ventilated torque converter cover. General lines are similar to those of the Gold Wing.

44

45

46

47

48

44. At a glance, the engine unit looks fairly conventional from this angle, but side stand linkage and adjuster give the game away.

45. The linkage, shown here in greater detail, is a safety device to prevent the machine from making unscheduled departures due to the effects of 'automatic creep'.

46. With the footrest raised, an unfamiliar shaft may be seen below and to the rear of the gearchange pedal. The black plastic cap is removed to reveal a kickstart shaft.

47. Below the seat was the emergency kickstart lever, stowed above the battery and near one of many warning stickers.

48. A view from the top showing the kickstart in position. Its unusual location on the left-hand side is due to the large torque converter fitted to the right-hand side of the unit.

49

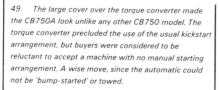

50

51

52

49.   The large cover over the torque converter made the CB750A look unlike any other CB750 model. The torque converter precluded the use of the usual kickstart arrangement, but buyers were considered to be reluctant to accept a machine with no manual starting arrangement. A wise move, since the automatic could not be 'bump-started' or towed.

50.   Because the automatic could not be left 'in gear' for hill parking on the prop stand, a parking brake

mechanism was incorporated. The release cable can be seen at the front of the unit.

51.   The parking brake is controlled by this choke-type knob which emerges on the left-hand side below the fuel tank.

52.   Part of the styling package was the extensive plated shrouding around the steering head. The headlamp is carried on a tubular subframe.

53

54

55

56

53. An unnerving sight to most motorcyclists – no clutch lever! In use the automatic was quite easy to ride, once the rider had adapted to an unfamiliar concept.

54. The instrument panel shows the dummy clock containing lights for neutral, Low and Drive, plus warning lights and fuel gauge. Speedometer incorporates range markings for the two forward ratios. Note combined ignition and steering lock.

55. The side panel emblem of what was perhaps the least popular and most interesting CB750.

56. Not a familiar sight on British roads, this Police model CB750 is another model from Dave Ayesthorpe's collection. It is based on the original model CB750.

57

58

59

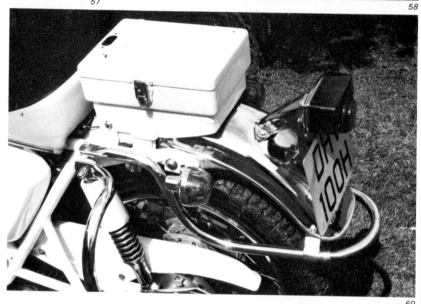

60

61

57.   Note the radio platform behind the special single seat. Rear crashbar is mounted at rear suspension top stud and fits in place of pillion footrest.

59.   Shown clearly in this view is the special headlamp nacelle incorporating the large calibrated speedometer required for police use. No tachometer is fitted. Front crashbar carries emergency lights and siren.

60.   Close up of crashbar shows the substantial lamp mounting. Tank is standard CB750, and at present is lacking its striping – Dave is trying to locate a suitable pattern for this.

60.   The rear bumper bar arrangement can be seen in this shot. Apart from these added chromium-plated items, brightwork is lacking on the Police model.

61.   Most of the machine is similar to the civilian CB750, but looks different in its white finish. The old familiar four-pipe exhaust is retained.

62

62. A smart two-tone single seat failed to tempt British forces to 'meet the nicest people'. It seems likely that buying Japanese during the declining years of the British industry would have been considered very poor taste.

63. Incorporated in the right-hand emergency lamp mounting is the substantial bracket which supports a very American siren.

64. The siren is clamped to mounting as shown. The very heavy cable drives the unit.

65. This massive roller arrangement is brought into contact with the tyre sidewall by a cable and lever (missing at present), driving the siren via the cable. History does not relate whether the road or the roller wore out rear tyres fastest.

63

64

65

66

67

68

66.   The right-hand handlebar controls, resplendent in polished alloy.

67.   The left-hand handlebar controls. Note that almost every switch is the reverse of normal practice.

68.   The large and legible Police-type speedometer, in KPH on this evaluation model. This is what the patrolman was to have used to apprehend speeding offenders, but for a while at least, the British Police continued to bike British.

C1

C2

C1. The exception that proved the rule. Eric Warburton's beautifully restored CB750 model disproves the popular adage that 'you never see an old Japanese bike'. Compare this with an equivalent modern Japanese four and the CB750 looks refreshingly clean and uncluttered. This particular machine has taken Eric many years and a great deal of money to complete, and must form an invaluable source of reference for future restorers.

C2. What dazzled in 1969 now seems to be subtle and understated. The clean lines of the tank are highlighted by the metal tank badge and quick-release filler cap. Decal design changed regularly over the years.

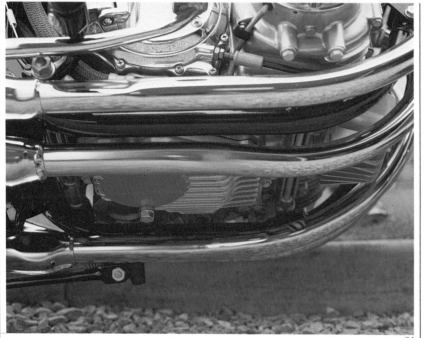

C3. Any CB750 owners reading this book may find the appearance of the engine hard to believe. Though notoriously difficult to keep clean, it **can** be done! Note the original side panel logo, and the painted air cleaner casing peculiar to the CB750 alone. Just visible is the outer carburettor's throttle cable – the four cable arrangement being another identifying feature of the original model.

C4. Yes, it really is this clean. View of underside of engine in which a wet sump is conspicuous by its absence. Just visible at the junction of the furthest pipe and silencer is the small drain hole which helps prevent silencer rotting – but only if it is kept clear.

C5.   This view of the handlebar area shows the instrumentation, looking almost European by current standards. Uncluttered clock faces incorporated warning lamps for main beam, indicators, oil pressure and neutral. The speedometer featured a standard odometer plus resettable trip meter.

C6.   Compare this left hand view of Eric Warburton's CB750K0 with the similar shot of his CB750, and there are few obvious differences, the K0 being a transitional model. Note that engine protection bars and mudflap are non-standard.

C5

C6

C7. Engine shot of CB750K0 shows new fluted type air cleaner casing and linkage-operated carburettors, standard features of subsequent models. Side panels and tank are the same as those of the CB750, but with revised paintwork.

C8. This view of the CB750K2 shows the newer type of side panel that characterises the 'K' series. New paintwork and decals are evident, as is the change from painted to chromium-plated fork shrouds. The K2 is probably the most generally familiar 'Honda 750' to most riders.

C9. On the K6 model, the warning lamps were incorporated in a one-piece handlebar clamp, together with a Honda logo. Ignition switch still resided just below the fuel tank at this stage. US product liability laws provoked the outbreak of 'caution' stickers, one of which is just visible at bottom of shot.

C10. One of many variations of handlebar switch – again on a K6 model. Note the twin throttle cables used to open and close the throttle valves via a pulley and linkage.

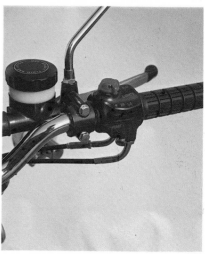

C7

C9

C8

C10

C11

C12

C13

C11. The latest styling job on the K series resulted in the K7. Note the lack of fork gaiters (boots) and the trim and logo on the lower yoke. The tank, side panels and seat reflect the styling revamp. Note also that the Honda wing emblem on the side panel has been replaced by the '750 Four K' emblem.

C12. A head-on view of the K7. Noticeable are the flat handlebars on this European model. Between the instruments is a small warning lamp nacelle.

C13. This publicity photograph shows the CB750F1 at the time of its launch. This was an attempt to make the ageing CB750 more sporting. Apart from obvious styling changes, note the four-into-one exhaust system. The model was to have replaced the K series, but the latter was reprieved by popular demand.

C14.   The F1 featured an hydraulic rear disc brake, in place of the drum unit fitted to all previous models. This also entailed the fitting of the alloy footrest hanger visible in C13.

C15.   Late models were equipped with a recessed fuel filler closed by a locking flap. This photograph shows an F2 model.

C16.   The last and sportiest CB750, the F2, was extensively modified as described in the text. Matt black was very much in vogue by then and even extended to the fork lower legs (sliders). Also new at the time were the composite 'Comstar' wheels. These worked well enough but never gained universal acceptance by the public – Honda now use cast wheels like everyone else.

C14

C15

C16

C17

C17. At a glance, this could be almost any late
CB750, but closer examination reveals extensive styling
changes, similar to the Gold Wing in some respects. The
side panel badge tells the full story – 750 Hondamatic.
This machine forms part of Dave Ayesthorpe's collection
of unusual Japanese models.

C18. Right-hand side of CB750 Automatic is
obviously different from all manual models, the large
ventilated cover housing the torque converter assembly.
Note also late pattern carburettors in which operating
links are internal.

C18

Super Profile

C19.   This rare Police model belongs to Dave Ayesthorpe and will be unfamiliar to most UK readers. The machine is one of the few used for evaluation, but they were never taken up by UK forces. This example is almost original and complete, but lacks tank stripes and one or two detail parts. Note standard equipment lights and friction driven siren on front crash bars.

C20.   In this left-hand view of the Police model note the extensive use of white enamel in place of polished or plated items. Radio pack mounts behind special single seat. Note also the engine crash bars and chrome support rail around the rear mudguard.

C19

C20